PURPOSE STUDY BIBLE
GENESIS

DR. JOHN W. STANKO

urbanpress

Purpose Study Bible: Genesis
by John W. Stanko
Copyright ©2021 John W. Stanko

ISBN 978-1-63360-160-4

For Worldwide Distribution
Printed in the U.S.A.

Urban Press
P.O. Box 8881
Pittsburgh, PA 15221-0881
412.646.2780
www.urbanpress.us

INTRODUCTION

It has been on my heart for quite some time to produce a *Purpose Study Bible*, similar to others on the market such as *The Spirit-Filled Bible, The Leadership Bible, The African Bible*, and *The Student Bible*. Each one of those incorporates insights about a particular topic for a target audience so there is commentary in the Bible to which users can easily refer. I wanted my *Purpose Study Bible* to focus on what I have labeled the five Gold Mine Principles, which are purpose, creativity, goal setting, time management, and faith. I have taught and written about those concepts since 1991 and wanted to produce a devotional study that would equip readers for purpose and productivity while giving them a devotional format. Part of my hesitancy to this point was determining exactly how I was going to format and then publish this Bible.

In 2019, I completed and published what I refer to as a devotional commentary covering every verse in the New Testament. I named that series *Live the Word* because my objective was to help readers not just become more familiar with the Word but also to apply and live it. To that end, I did not produce a technical study but rather an easy-to-read work that included questions readers can ask themselves to assist in the application process. So readers would not miss those questions, I put them in bold in the hope those questions would "jump out" at them. Every one of those studies is posted online so they are available free of charge to people the world over since some do not have the ability to purchase print copies.

Since I have completed my New Testament study, it's now time to dive into the Old Testament using the same format and begin the *Purpose Study Bible*. I will not produce a verse-by-verse study as I did with my New Testament commentary. Instead, I will go chapter by chapter and will focus only on passages that address some specific aspect of the Gold Mine Principles. There will be some chapters that will have a few entries while other chapters are skipped altogether. I will once again post these studies online so they will be available to any and all at www.stankobiblestudy.com.

Also, as I did with *Live the Word*, I will publish the *Purpose Study Bible* in volumes, starting with Genesis—the volume you hold in your hand. I have no idea how many volumes this *Study Bible* will require, and I am hoping God will grant me enough days to complete this work. That is up to Him, but I will do my part and give myself to write as He gives me strength.

Genesis

It made sense to start with Genesis as the first book in this *Purpose Study Bible*. In this volume, there are 51 entries generated from the 50 chapters in Genesis. However, that is not how all these studies will be—approximately one entry for each chapter. There are 920 chapters in the Old Testament but there may be 1,000, or 800, or 1,200 entries. I will make that up as I go along.

As with *Live the Word*, I have included questions in bold for you to consider as you reflect on what I wrote about the Gold Mine Principles. Other than that, there is nothing special to look for or trends that emerged. The five Gold Mine Principles all had their genesis (pardon the pun) in the first book of the Bible, which makes their study an important foundation for understanding and applying them. I consider this *Study Bible* another devotional of sorts, so I hope you will approach it as such, as well as a means by which you can be equipped for a purposeful lifestyle.

I pray you enjoy reading these studies as much as I enjoyed writing them, and I also pray they will equip and empower you for purposeful and fruitful work as you express your creativity in the days and years ahead. Thank you for reading and may the Lord bless the study and reading of His word in volume one of the *Purpose Study Bible.*

John W. Stanko
Pittsburgh, PA USA
February 2021

STUDY 1

ORDER
OUT OF CHAOS
GENESIS 1:2

Welcome to the start of this Bible commentary on the topics of purpose and creativity in the Bible. We start at the beginning, not only of the Bible, but where purpose began for me:

> Now the earth was formless and empty, darkness was over the surface of the deep, and the Spirit of God was hovering over the waters (Genesis 1:2).

I noticed this verse when I was a young man and turned to a Bible commentary to read more about it. The author wrote "the Spirit was present to bring order out of chaos." Those words jumped out at me and have become the summary of my life purpose with one small adjustment: my purpose is "to *create* order out of chaos." Those few words perfectly summarize who I am and what I have done all my adult life.

There is a Bible verse, passage, chapter, or book that

summarizes and describes who you are as well. **Do you know what or where it is? What does it say about you? If you know, are you being true to its meaning?** If you do not know, then be watching and waiting. You may not recognize it right now, but one day you will be reading the Word, and your biblical purpose will literally jump off the page as mine did many years ago. Remember, the goal is a simple statement of purpose with some biblical justification or definition to go with it.

STUDY 2

IN HIS IMAGE
GENESIS 1:26-27

Let's look at the concept of creativity as described in Genesis 1:26-27:

> Then God said, "Let us make mankind in our image, in our likeness, so that they may rule over the fish in the sea and the birds in the sky, over the livestock and all the wild animals, and over all the creatures that move along the ground." So God created mankind in his own image, in the image of God he created them; male and female he created them.

Throughout Genesis 1, we see God portrayed as the Creator, deliberately making His creation on a day-by-day basis. Then God decided, in His infinite wisdom, to create mankind, but distinguished them from all His other creatures by making them "in our image and likeness." Once God decided to create, He did not put it off or procrastinate, He immediately set about to create mankind "in His own image" (that phrase was mentioned twice for emphasis).

Theologians have debated what part of mankind reflects God's image, but in this context, let's focus on creativity. The Creator made us to be creative, and we are little creative machines, producing body chemicals, dreams, new cells, ideas, sentences, written and verbal communication, and a host of other daily activities that are creative. In fact, you will probably utter a sentence today that has never been spoken before in the history of mankind in just the way you spoke it.

Do you take your creativity for granted, or do you receive and express it as an important aspect of who God created you to be? What more can you do to reflect His image in what you create? Is your creativity to be a hobby or to receive front-and-center attention in your life's work and daily routine?

STUDY 3

FIRST SIGN OF PURPOSE
GENESIS 1:28

The concept of life purpose is found in the earliest verses of the Bible:

> God blessed them and said to them, "Be fruitful and increase in number; fill the earth and subdue it. Rule over the fish in the sea and the birds in the sky and over every living creature that moves on the ground" (Genesis 1:28).

This verse contains what many refer to as the dominion mandate. God commissioned the first humans He created to do purposeful work He would assign, and that would involve them increasing in number and exercising control over His creation. God's creation at first was mostly agricultural, but it would eventually extend to the major spheres of life like business, government, education, the military, ministry, and communication.

Notice that God blessed them when He spoke purpose into their lives and you are blessed when you find and fulfill your purpose. Your purpose is not to attend church or to simply work and make a living. You are here to do more than eat, play, breed, and sleep. You have a purpose: something for you to do that only you can do, something to be that only you can be.

Do you see that purpose precedes the Fall of man, and that means Jesus came to restore the vitality and importance of purpose in the lives of each one of His people? Do you know what your purpose is? What price are you willing to pay to discover it? What price are you willing to pay to fulfill it?

STUDY 4

OUR PROVISION
GENESIS 1:29-30

After the Lord gave us purpose, He then promised to meet our every need:

> Then God said, "I give you every seed-bearing plant on the face of the whole earth and every tree that has fruit with seed in it. They will be yours for food. And to all the beasts of the earth and all the birds in the sky and all the creatures that move along the ground—everything that has the breath of life in it—I give every green plant for food." And it was so (Genesis 1:29-30).

Notice that God did not say we would work for our food. Instead, He assigned us work but then promised to *give* us our food. That means our food and provision are gifts and not wages. This flies in the face of culture that says we must work and get paid by an employer. Instead, God directs us to do His work and He promises to pay us. That frees us from doing things simply for the money so we can pursue our individual purpose, trusting God for what we need. Jesus reiterated this promise when He directed us to "seek first His kingdom" and all that we need—food, clothing, shelter, transportation—would be provided for us (see Matthew 6:33).

Are you a slave to your work because that is the only way you believe God can provide for you? Do you see that your income is a gift from God and not the result of your work contract? Do you see this means God is your provider and not your employer? Armed with this truth, what adjustments can you make in your thinking and then in your approach to work and the provision you need for life?

STUDY 5

GOD RESTED
GENESIS 2:1-3

When God had finished His creative work, we read this report:

> Thus the heavens and the earth were completed, and all their hosts. By the seventh day God completed His work which He had done, and He rested on the seventh day from all His work which He had done. Then God blessed the seventh day and sanctified it, because in it He rested from all His work which God had created and made (Genesis 2:1-3).

People have developed a doctrine of the Sabbath from these verses. The Hebrew word for *rested* in verses two and three is *sahabat*. The doctrine maintains God sanctified the day as a pattern for man to follow. Yet God did not need to rest because He was tired; He rested because He saw that His work was good or complete: "God saw all that He had made, and behold, it was very good. And there was evening and there was morning, the sixth day" (Genesis 1:31).

The New Testament sheds more light on this concept of rest in Hebrews 4:

> Therefore, since the promise of entering his rest still stands, let us be careful that none of you be found to have fallen short of it. For we also have had the good news proclaimed to us, just as they did; but the message they heard was of no value to them, because they did not share the faith of those who obeyed. Now we who have believed enter that rest, just as God has said, "So I declared on oath in my anger, 'They shall never enter my rest.'" [see Psalm 95:11.] And yet his works have been finished since the creation of the world. For somewhere he has spoken about the seventh day in these words: "On the seventh day God rested from all his works." And again in the passage above he says, "They shall never enter my rest" (Hebrews 4:1-5).

Jesus was clear that the Sabbath was instituted for people and not for God: "Then he said to them, 'The Sabbath was made for man, not man for the Sabbath'" (Mark 2:27).

Could there be a meaning in the Sabbath that we have not considered? Could it be to step back and enjoy what we have created and the purpose work we have done? Did God intend for people to slave for six days and then take a nap on the seventh day so they can resume their brutal, debilitating labor?

Could the Sabbath be for us to keep from being driven by work but to reflect on our enjoyment of it and our fruit from it? If you don't enjoy your work, do you believe that is God's will for your life? If that is your assumption, then consider this verse: "A person can do nothing better than to eat and drink and find satisfaction in their own toil. This too, I see, is from the hand of God" (Ecclesiastes 2:24).

STUDY 6

GOD THE ARTIST
GENESIS 2:8-9

Not only did God create but God created well, and that included beauty, symmetry, and taste:

> Now the Lord God had planted a garden in the east, in Eden; and there he put the man he had formed. The Lord God made all kinds of trees grow out of the ground—trees that were pleasing to the eye and good for food. In the middle of the garden were the tree of life and the tree of the knowledge of good and evil (Genesis 2:8-9).

When the Lord planted a garden, He paid attention to how the garden looked and how it tasted. That indicates God is interested in beauty, color, shape, diversity, order, and structure. Not only that, but God created man with taste, otherwise why would God have made the food in the garden good to eat? That means those people who give themselves to gardening, cooking, or artistic endeavors pleasing to the eye and in "good taste" honor and glorify God by following His example. Later we will see, however, that man decided to eat of the wrong tree (the tree of the knowledge of good and evil) and that meant people and not God would be the ultimate judge of beauty and art. Those things no longer existed to glorify God but instead to express mankind's fallen nature and rebellion.

Do you appreciate not only nature but the other aspects of God's creation He made like culture, language, economics, fashion, culinary arts, and diverse artistic endeavors? Are you being creative in the image of God as He would have you do? Do you have a theology of creativity that grounds it in God's will and purpose for your life, thus making it more of a calling and less of an optional hobby or diversion? What more can you do to be creative as part of your purpose mandate?

GARDEN ASSIGNMENT
GENESIS 2:15-17

After God created, He gave man an assignment and placed him in the Garden:

> The Lord God took the man and put him in the Garden of Eden to work it and take care of it. And the Lord God commanded the man, "You are free to eat from any tree in the garden; but you must not eat from the tree of the knowledge of good and evil, for when you eat from it you will certainly die" (Genesis 2:15-17).

In this passage, we learn that man once existed outside the Garden for God took and placed him there. That indicates God assigns us the sphere of His creation where He wants us to be so we can "take care of it." Then God gave man freedom to eat whatever He wanted to eat from any tree except one:

the tree of the knowledge of good and evil. God then set the consequences if man, in his freedom, ever chose to disobey. That consequence involved death, decay, and misery.

We see here that God gave man purpose along with freedom to structure and plan his work as he saw fit while God directed the work. This Garden was not to be the end of God's creation, but only its beginning. It was man's job not only to care for it but to expand and develop it as the number of people increased and man's creativity impacted his environment to bring about technology and the systems of existence. This included things like education, government, business, the arts, and worship.'

Are you working in the portion of the Garden where God assigned you? Are you expressing His creativity He placed in you? Do you work for the Lord and trust Him to give you the food He promised, or do you work for money? Do you enjoy your work and the freedom God designed you to have to structure it as you think best? If you answered no to any of those questions (or don't know the answers), then perhaps it is time to ask yourself where you need to be and what it will take to get you connected to your Garden assignment.

STUDY 8

YOUR CREATIVITY
GENESIS 2:18-21

It became clear that if man was going to tend the Garden, he was going to need suitable helpers. Therefore, we read,

> The Lord God said, "It is not good for the man to be alone. I will make a helper suitable for him." Now the Lord God had formed out of the ground all the wild animals and all the birds in the sky. He brought them to the man to see what he would name them; and whatever the man called each living creature, that was its name. So the man gave names to all the livestock, the birds in the sky and all the wild animals. But for Adam no suitable helper was found (Genesis 2:18-21).

As stated in a previous study, God directed Adam's work, but Adam was free to structure and complete the work as he saw fit. In this instance, God brought the animals for Adam to name. God did not tell Adam what to name them. He did not lay on his heart or whisper in his ear what the name was to be;

it was up to Adam to express his creativity.

Jesus came to reconcile all things to God, which includes man's purpose and his creativity. He did not come to control humans but rather He came to make them all they were created and intended to be before the Fall. That means God gave us our ability to create and now expects us to express it in the context of our Garden purpose. That also means your creative talents are not to be a hobby or something you do when you have time but are to be front and center in your work and life.

Do you consider yourself a creative person? If not, why not? Perhaps the problem is your definition of creativity? Do you see time management, problem solving, raising children, and planning a vacation as creative expressions? You don't have to paint like Rembrandt, write like Hemingway, or compose like Mozart to be considered creative.

Therefore, what are your creative expressions? How often do you express them? Have you submitted them to God so He can direct them while you work to make them all they can be to bring Him glory by using them regularly? Has fear robbed you of your ability to create?

TEAMWORK
GENESIS 2:20-25

After Adam expressed his creativity by naming the animals, his next lesson was about teamwork:

> So the man gave names to all the livestock, the birds in the sky and all the wild animals. But for Adam no suitable helper was found. So the Lord God caused the man to fall into a deep sleep; and while he was sleeping, he took one of the man's ribs and then closed up the place with flesh. Then the Lord God made a woman from the rib he had taken out of the man, and he brought her to the man. The man said, "This is now bone of my bones and flesh of my flesh; she shall be called 'woman,' for she was taken out of man." That is why a man leaves his father and mother and is united to his wife, and they become one flesh. Adam and his wife were both naked, and they felt no shame (Genesis 2:20-25).

The work God had assigned Adam could not be done

alone so God created a helper "suitable to him" after He had already ordered him "to be fruitful and to multiply" (Genesis 1:28a). This meant there would be many other helpers needed to "rule over the fish in the sea and the birds in the sky and over every living creature that moves on the ground" (Genesis 1:28b). This introduced the concept of teamwork, which would eventually have to go beyond husbands, wives, and families to include a host of others—all uniquely gifted to contribute something to man's dominion mandate. It is of note that Adam and Eve felt no shame in one another's presence, but we will revisit this concept of shame again after the Fall.

The New Testament painted a clearer picture of the concept of teamwork when Paul introduced the concept of spiritual gifts and roles in the body of Christ. He expanded on the need for teams, but that need was first expressed here in Genesis 2. **Are you part of anyone's team, whether in ministry, work, or some other expression of the dominion mandate? What are the strengths you bring to the team? Is the objective of your work and teamwork clear to you and others? How well do you know your teammates?**

FEAR AND SHAME
GENESIS 3:8-10

Immediately after Adam and Eve ate of the forbidden tree, this is how they reacted:

> Then the man and his wife heard the sound of the Lord God as he was walking in the garden in the cool of the day, and they hid from the Lord God among the trees of the garden. But the Lord God called to the man, "Where are you?" He answered, "I heard you in the garden, and I was afraid because I was naked; so I hid" (Genesis 3:8-10).

We read in Genesis 2:25 that "Adam and his wife were both naked, and they felt no shame." Then they fell from grace and we read that they were afraid and felt shame, realizing they were naked. This led to the almost humorous scenario where they tried to hide from the Lord among the trees of the Garden. We are the children of Adam and Eve and we are also hiding, sometimes even in the Church, because we are self-conscious and overcome with feelings of terror due to our inadequacy and separation from God. In Genesis 2, God had spoken to Adam and he responded without fear. After he sinned, Adam heard God and hid.

Fear and shame that cause us to hide are usually still our first reactions to the concepts of purpose and creativity. We are afraid of getting ahead of the Lord, of missing the Lord, of failure, of success, of what others will say and do. When we step out to create, we tend to minimize what we have done because we are ashamed of what we have produced. What's more, the fear and shame mask themselves as rational and even spiritual responses that seem normal and acceptable to us and God.

Where and how are shame and fear robbing you of the chance to fulfill your purpose and express your creativity? Assume fear is blocking your way even if you don't agree or see that it is. Ask God, **"Am I afraid?"** Keep looking for usually there is fear or shame somewhere that is holding you back. When you discover the fear, simply bring it to the light and expose it for what it is and it will set you free. If you continue to allow fear to masquerade as something else, you will be content to watch others express the will of God for their lives while you stay hidden from yours.

STUDY 11

ENMITY
GENESIS 3:14-15

After Adam and Eve ate of the forbidden tree, the Lord spelled out the consequences for their deed, starting with the serpent:

> "Cursed are you above all livestock and all wild animals! You will crawl on your belly and you will eat dust all the days of your life. And I will put enmity between you and the woman, and between your offspring and hers; he will crush your head, and you will strike his heel" (Genesis 3:14-15).

The Lord addressed the serpent who had human qualities of understanding and communication. It is obvious that the serpent represented Satan and his kingdom. The Lord promised to put "enmity" between his kingdom and the woman's offspring, which is another word for hostility or hatred. That promise has certainly come to pass.

> Then from his mouth the serpent spewed water like a river, to overtake the woman and sweep her away

with the torrent. But the earth helped the woman by opening its mouth and swallowing the river that the dragon had spewed out of his mouth. Then the dragon was enraged at the woman and went off to wage war against the rest of her offspring—those who keep God's commands and hold fast their testimony about Jesus (Revelation 12:15-17).

This passage in Genesis 3 also includes the first proclamation of the gospel of Christ, for God promised to act in such a manner that the woman and her offspring would be victorious over their enemy through one of the woman's offspring which we know to be Jesus. This is also confirmed in the Revelation 12 passage.

This hatred or enmity is certainly present when anyone seeks to express their God-given purpose or express their creativity, and the intensity of the opposition can cause people to doubt or hesitate as they move forward. This then gives rise to fear that they have missed the Lord or are out of His will. **Have you experienced this kind of spiritual opposition? Are you surprised by the intensity? Do you fight back with the weapons you have at your disposal?**

> Finally, be strong in the Lord and in his mighty power. Put on the full armor of God, so that you can take your stand against the devil's schemes. For our struggle is not against flesh and blood, but against the rulers, against the authorities, against the powers of this dark world and against the spiritual forces of evil in the heavenly realms (Ephesians 6:10-12).

If you are going to realize your full potential in Christ, you must be ready to do battle in a war you did not start but were drafted into when you made a commitment to Christ.

TWO TREES
GENESIS 2:9, 3:22-24

There are two trees that figure prominently in the Genesis story. One is the tree of the knowledge of good and evil and other is the tree of eternal life:

> The Lord God made all kinds of trees grow out of the ground—trees that were pleasing to the eye and good for food. In the middle of the garden were the tree of life and the tree of the knowledge of good and evil (Genesis 2:9).

> And the Lord God said, "The man has now become like one of us, knowing good and evil. He must not be allowed to reach out his hand and take also from the tree of life and eat, and live forever." So the Lord God banished him from the Garden of Eden to work the ground from which he had been taken. After he drove the man out, he placed on the east side of the Garden of Eden cherubim and a flaming sword flashing back and forth to guard the way to the tree of life

(Genesis 3:22-24).

Adam and Eve ate from the tree of the knowledge of good and evil. This meant they would no longer rely on God's interpretation of good and evil; instead, they would substitute their own standard. They would decide what was good and not good, and we see that play out in society all day every day. People decide what they want to do, how they will do it, and then label the results good or bad. This means what God considers good is often considered not good and vice versa.

Once the couple was in their fallen state, God could not allow them to eat from the eternal life tree (which they were permitted to eat from prior to their sin). If they had done so, they would have existed in their fallen state forever with no way of escape. Therefore, God posted a guard to keep man from accessing that eternal life fruit, and that tree was only made available later through Christ.

These two trees have implications for you as they relate to your purpose and creativity. No longer can you alone be the judge of your assigned purpose or your expressed creativity, deciding whether they are good or not good. You must learn to trust the Lord and rely on His perspective of who you are, rejecting fear and shame (products of the tree of the knowledge of good and evil) and drawing on the life found in Christ.

Are you ready to surrender your desire to judge who you are and the work you do according to your own perspective? Are you willing to trust in the standards presented in God's word for what is good and evil? Can you rely on God's direction for your life's work and not take matters into your own hands by judging according to the world's standard of right and wrong?

AFTER THE FALL
GENESIS 4:1-2

As we move into Genesis 4, we read that Adam and Eve got on with their lives after the cataclysmic events surrounding their Fall from grace:

> Adam made love to his wife Eve, and she became pregnant and gave birth to Cain. She said, "With the help of the Lord I have brought forth a man." Later she gave birth to his brother Abel. Now Abel kept flocks, and Cain worked the soil (Genesis 4:1-2).

Before we proceed, let's consider what has happened so far and the implications. We have looked at five concepts present in the first three chapters of the Bible:

1. We saw that Adam and Eve had direct **fellowship with God** who spoke with them face to face.

2. God directed their work in accord with His desire that they multiply and have dominion over the earth, which was their **purpose**.

3. While God directed their work, Adam and Eve injected their **creativity** into what they did.

4. Eve was created to work alongside Adam to form a creative and purposeful **team**.

5. The first family was to **rest** on the seventh day, not because they were exhausted but so they could refocus and enjoy the fruit of their labors.

When our parents sinned, each concept was impacted by their sin but not eliminated. They were still expected to be purposeful, have fellowship with their Maker, be a creative team, and rest. As time went on, each aspect became more complicated and difficult to carry out until they were totally obscured or buried under centuries of sin residue.

The good news is Jesus came not only to restore our fellowship with God but also to restore God's intent of how things were to be *before* the Fall. In other words, Jesus came to restore our ability to be purposeful, creative, work in teams, and truly rest from our own works (and that is not to lie on a hammock and do nothing):

> And he is the head of the body, the church; he is the beginning and the firstborn from among the dead, so that in everything he might have the supremacy. For God was pleased to have all his fullness dwell in him, and through him to reconcile to himself *all things*, whether things on earth or things in heaven, by making peace through his blood, shed on the cross (Colossians 1:18-20, emphasis added).

Have you ever given any thought to the fact that Jesus, who is the second Adam (see Romans 5:12-21), came to restore the Garden scenario in our lives? Are you allowing Christ to reconcile, restore, and activate every aspect of your being, or are you only expecting spiritual and not purpose restoration? Are you actively seeking to understand your God-given purpose and creativity?

Do you realize that your limitations require you to work in a team setting, whether in a family, ministry, or work setting, relying on other's strengths while you contribute yours? Are you resting in your work as you enjoy your fruit and the fact that you are doing God's will right where you are?

STUDY 14

DIVERSITY OF PURPOSE
GENESIS 4:19-22

After Adam and Eve sinned, life on Earth began to expand but the elements introduced in the pre-Fall days were still in effect, including purpose:

> Lamech married two women, one named Adah and the other Zillah. Adah gave birth to Jabal; he was the father of those who live in tents and raise livestock. His brother's name was Jubal; he was the father of all who play stringed instruments and pipes. Zillah also had a son, Tubal-Cain, who forged all kinds of tools out of bronze and iron. Tubal-Cain's sister was Naamah (Genesis 4:19-22).

Notice from this passage the diversity of interests and skills that emerged. One was a shepherd, one a musician, and another a blacksmith or metal worker. I wonder how they knew what they were to do with their lives? It was simple, as it is today: each one followed his or her interests and that led them right where they needed to be. Also, it seems that each person then passed on their skills and interests to others so that entire industries or areas of labor were introduced and continued through the generations (not only to family members but to other interested and skilled individuals).

There had to be creativity expressed in each of these areas as people pioneered their work and learned how to be productive. What's more, God was with them because this was His intent from the beginning—that each person would fulfill His dominion mandate described in Genesis 1:28: "God blessed them and said to them, 'Be fruitful and increase in number; fill the earth and subdue it. Rule over the fish in the sea and the birds in the sky and over every living creature that moves on the ground.'"

What is your area of interest in life? Have you pursued it to the extent that you can be proficient, learning to master that area? Has fear kept you from doing that? Are you teaching others, imparting the skills and knowledge you have amassed in your area of expertise? What more can you do to become absorbed in your work or to be more effective in passing it on to others? What would people say is your legacy as they behold your life and work?

NOAH'S CREATIVITY
GENESIS 6:5-8, 15-16

As stated earlier, the concepts introduced in the earliest chapters of Genesis were still in effect after the Fall (things like purpose, creativity, and teamwork), but they were so infected by sin that eventually they became completely alienated from the Lord. Therefore, the Lord needed to "reboot" the human race as we read in Genesis 6:

> The Lord saw how great the wickedness of the human race had become on the earth, and that every inclination of the thoughts of the human heart was only evil all the time. The Lord regretted that he had made human beings on the earth, and his heart was deeply troubled. So the Lord said, "I will wipe from the face of the earth the human race I have created—and with them the animals, the birds and the creatures that move along the ground—for I regret that I have made them." But Noah found favor in the eyes of the Lord (Genesis 6:5-8).

In order to start over, God gave Noah a set of plans to build an ark. Keep in mind that Noah had never seen rain and no one had ever built an ark before:

> "This is how you are to build it: The ark is to be three hundred cubits long, fifty cubits wide and thirty cubits high. Make a roof for it, leaving below the roof an opening one cubit high all around. Put a door in the side of the ark and make lower, middle and upper decks" (Genesis 6:15-16).

Those verses beg the question: How did Noah know how to build an ark? You may respond, "God told him how to do it," but is that accurate? After all, if someone gave you the plans to build a five-story building and you were not an architect or construction worker, would you be able to build it? Probably not. The point is that Noah had a skill, maybe even a gift, to build and he expressed his creativity to construct the ark.

Do you have any creative skills that seem so natural that you think anyone could do what comes easily to you? Can you read a pattern and create a dress? Read instructions and put together a bicycle? Learn a language quickly and easily by listening to a step-by-step guide?

If you can do any of those things or a myriad of other similar things, then you have unique creativity that is not an accident—it is something God equipped you to do. Therefore, you should take it more seriously than you have up to this point in your life. **If you are to take it more seriously, what should you do? School? Reading? Find a mentor or coach? Get busy creating?** Whatever it is, stop wasting this skill or gift (or whatever you label it) and start being more creative than you have ever been.

A LONG-TERM GOAL
GENESIS 6:19-21

God directed Noah to build an ark and then gave him these instructions:

> "You are to bring into the ark two of all living creatures, male and female, to keep them alive with you. Two of every kind of bird, of every kind of animal and of every kind of creature that moves along the ground will come to you to be kept alive. You are to take every kind of food that is to be eaten and store it away as food for you and for them" (Genesis 6:19-21).

What do these instructions tell us about Noah and his work?

1. The ark probably took between 50-70 years to construct.

2. Noah could not have built it himself; he had to organize his family to do the work with him.

3. His family had to have some construction skills

in order to help.

4. Once built, Noah had to organize the way forward by gathering food and receiving the animals. (Note that he did not have to go fetch the animals; God brought them to him.)

5. Noah, like Adam and Eve, worked in partnership with God. God directed the work, but Noah had to draw on his gifts and intelligence to complete the task.

6. Noah had to have faith in God to begin and complete the task. Faith has always been a requirement to please and serve God.

7. Noah had to learn how to manage his time to get the job done.

Some significant projects and accomplishments cannot be achieved in a short period of time. They also require thought and creativity in order to reach the goal. I just completed an 18-year project of writing and then publishing a New Testament commentary. That required me to apply the same practices Noah used as described above.

Do you have any long-term goals? Do you have something in which you can invest the best of who you are and who God made you to be? Do you feel like God is directing your work? Are you responding by utilizing your energy, gifts, and talent?

STUDY 17

STARTING OVER
GENESIS 9:1-3

After the Flood when the waters subsided, Noah, his family, and the animals disembarked from the Ark, and God gave them these instructions:

> Then God blessed Noah and his sons, saying to them, "Be fruitful and increase in number and fill the earth. The fear and dread of you will fall on all the beasts of the earth, and on all the birds in the sky, on every creature that moves along the ground, and on all the fish in the sea; they are given into your hands. Everything that lives and moves about will be food for you. Just as I gave you the green plants, I now give you everything" (Genesis 9:1-3).

Notice He told them exactly what He had told Adam and Eve—they were to "be fruitful, increase, and fill the earth." God also gave them not only the green plants for food, but also all creatures that moved. He gave them everything and the emphasis here is on the word *give*.

God was not telling Noah's family they were not to work. The work mandate was still in place, but they were not to have the mentality they had to work for their food or they would starve. God was their Provider, would guide their work, and would make sure they were taken care of.

Jesus, who came to restore things as they were in the Garden, addressed this issue of provision on more than one occasion. Let's look at one of His teachings on the subject:

> "Therefore I tell you, do not worry about your life, what you will eat or drink; or about your body, what you will wear. Is not life more than food, and the body more than clothes? Look at the birds of the air; they do not sow or reap or store away in barns, and yet your heavenly Father feeds them. Are you not much more valuable than they? Can any one of you by worrying add a single hour to your life?

> "And why do you worry about clothes? See how the flowers of the field grow. They do not labor or spin. Yet I tell you that not even Solomon in all his splendor was dressed like one of these. If that is how God clothes the grass of the field, which is here today and tomorrow is thrown into the fire, will he not much more clothe you—you of little faith? So do not worry, saying, 'What shall we eat?' or 'What shall we drink?' or 'What shall we wear?' For the pagans run after all these things, and your heavenly Father knows that you need them. But seek first his kingdom and his righteousness, and all these things will be given to you as well. Therefore do not worry about tomorrow, for tomorrow will worry about itself. Each day has enough trouble of its own" (Matthew 6:25-34).

Are you worrying over the state of the economy and your ability to feed you family? Are your thoughts and actions in alignment with what Jesus said—that if you seek to follow the King in His Kingdom, He will provide all you need (not necessarily all you want)?

What steps must you take or what attitudes must you adopt to be more focused in your work and less focused on your provision?

Please note: I am not suggesting you don't have to work. You do, but I am suggesting you not see your employer or job as your provider. God is your Provider and if you have to start over in another part of His "Garden" for work, He will take care of you along the way.

STUDY 18

SPREAD OUT
GENESIS 10:8-11

The Lord told Noah and his sons to "be fruitful and increase in number and fill the earth" (Genesis 9:1). Here is an example of how they and the generations following them responded:

> Cush was the father of Nimrod, who became a mighty warrior on the earth. He was a mighty hunter before the Lord; that is why it is said, "Like Nimrod, a mighty hunter before the Lord." The first centers of his kingdom were Babylon, Uruk, Akkad and Kalneh, in Shinar. From that land he went to Assyria, where he built Nineveh, Rehoboth Ir, Calah and Resen, which is between Nineveh and Calah—which is the great city (Genesis 10:8-11).

Obeying God's command, some went out and built cities and kingdoms, being true to their interests and purpose—like Nimrod who was a "mighty hunter before the Lord." These men did not necessarily honor or glorify God through their efforts, but they went out nonetheless and bore fruit, building kingdoms and establishing population centers that are mentioned throughout the Bible. Later, Jesus gave a similar command found in Matthew 28:19-20:

> "Therefore go and make disciples of all nations, baptizing them in the name of the Father and of the Son and of the Holy Spirit, and teaching them to obey everything I have commanded you. And surely I am with you always, to the very end of the age."

What are you doing with Jesus' command? Are you going? Are you helping others to go? Are you praying? Are you doing something in response to the command to spread out and bear fruit?

> "You did not choose me, but I chose you and appointed you so that you might go and bear fruit— fruit that will last—and so that whatever you ask in my name the Father will give you" (John 15:16).

It is important to understand that Genesis 10 and Matthew 28 are not simply directives to evangelize but to fulfill one's purpose, whatever that God-assigned purpose may be. **Are you fulfilling your purpose and bearing fruit? If so, what is your fruit?**

BUILDING A TOWER
GENESIS 11:1-4

We saw in Genesis 10 how people spread out to fill the earth as the Lord had commanded them to do. In Genesis 11, we read about those who stopped spreading out and instead decided to stay put and build a tower:

> Now the whole world had one language and a common speech. As people moved eastward, they found a plain in Shinar and settled there. They said to each other, "Come, let's make bricks and bake them thoroughly." They used brick instead of stone, and tar for mortar. Then they said, "Come, let us build ourselves a city, with a tower that reaches to the heavens, so that we may make a name for ourselves; otherwise we will be scattered over the face of the whole earth" (Genesis 11:1-4).

These people wanted to make "a name for themselves" and they determined to do it at any cost. What did they do? They made bricks. They lived in a hot climate, but decided to bake the bricks thoroughly, which meant they had to build fires—making an already unpleasant work environment even worse. Then they decided to use tar to hold the bricks together. Do you know what tar smells like when it's heated? It gives off a foul odor.

Contrast these conditions with those in the Garden and you will see what the Fall cost people in regard to their purpose and creativity and how they would ultimately be expressed. What's more, rather than spread *out* as they were commanded, these people decided to *stay* in one place and build *up*, believing they could reach heaven through their own effort and work.

Proverbs 13:15 states, "Good understanding giveth favour: but the way of transgressors is hard" (KJV) while Psalm 127:1-2 reports, "Unless the Lord builds the house, the builders labor in vain. Unless the Lord watches over the city, the guards stand watch in vain. In vain you rise early and stay up late, toiling for food to eat—for he grants sleep to those he loves."

How would you characterize your work and career? Do you enjoy your work or are you toiling away in the heat of the day in unpleasant conditions? Are you building a name for yourself or glorifying God?

Have you stubbornly planted yourself in one place, perhaps enduring mistreatment and a harsh environment rather than move on to something else? If you are making bricks in the desert, can you trust the Lord for something better? How will you find it?

POWER IN TEAMS
GENESIS 11:5-6

The story of the tower in Genesis 11 is important because it encapsulates and explains so many of the challenges we face as we build and function in teams and families. Let's look at how the Lord responded to their efforts to build a tower:

> But the Lord came down to see the city and the tower the people were building. The Lord said, "If as one people speaking the same language they have begun to do this, then nothing they plan to do will be impossible for them. (Genesis 11:5-6).

The people thought they were building a great edifice that would reach unto heaven. Yet the account says the Lord "came down" to see the city and the tower. (This shows that the people were doing more than building a tower; they were establishing a life center with the tower as the crowning achievement.) The Lord was not impressed with either for He had to "come down" to see them.

No matter how great our efforts, they are futile in God's

sight without His involvement and protection:

> "All of us have become like one who is unclean, and all our righteous acts are like filthy rags; we all shrivel up like a leaf, and like the wind our sins sweep us away. No one calls on your name or strives to lay hold of you; for you have hidden your face from us and have given us over to our sins" (Isaiah 64:6-7).

This is especially true of any works we do to try and gain His approval or earn His favor. We already have both, so our efforts should not be to gain God's favor, but to indicate we already enjoy His favor.

Notice also the power God put into the power of teams working together. He created us to feed off one another's gifts and strengths, and when we combine them for the right reasons, our efforts are greater as a whole than the sum of their individual parts. In other words, when we work together, one plus one can equal five or ten or more. That is the power of something called synergy. God had to thwart the synergy in this story because He had promised not to intervene again as He had during the Flood. Therefore, He had to prevent the builders from being successful for their own good and protection—or they would have kept building.

Are you working for the Lord or building a monument for yourself or your organization? (Even people working in ministry can be building something great for the wrong reasons.) **Are you part of a team that is experiencing synergy or one that is simply a collection of individuals working in silos or alone? What can you do to improve your team's dynamics and effectiveness?**

FAILURE
TO COMMUNICATE
GENESIS 11:7-9

As we look at the last lesson from the Tower of Babel, we see how the Lord thwarted the efforts of the people to settle down and build themselves a city with a monument:

> "Come, let us go down and confuse their language so they will not understand each other." So the Lord scattered them from there over all the earth, and they stopped building the city. That is why it was called Babel—because there the Lord confused the language of the whole world. From there the Lord scattered them over the face of the whole earth" (Genesis 11:7-9).

What exactly happened here? Did people suddenly start speaking different languages? There is the possibility that a few languages emerged from this story, but it is also possible that the Lord confused the language the people were already speaking so their singular goal became unclear or unsatisfactory. **Have you ever been totally confused by someone even though they were speaking your native tongue? Have you talked to someone using a common word but realized during the conversation that you both understood the word differently?** That can be a source of frustration and friction between people, causing them not to be "on the same page" with one another and preventing them from successfully working together.

This story tells us that God is involved not only in the development of human language, but also in enhancing communication between people—whether one-on-one or in a group. This truth is demonstrated in the story of Acts 2 when the Holy Spirit was poured out on the disciples:

> When the day of Pentecost came, they were all together in one place. Suddenly a sound like the blowing of a violent wind came from heaven and filled the whole house where they were sitting. They saw what seemed to be tongues of fire that separated and came to rest on each of them. All of them were filled with the Holy Spirit and began to speak in other tongues as the Spirit enabled them.
>
> Now there were staying in Jerusalem God-fearing Jews from every nation under heaven. When they heard this sound, a crowd came together in bewilderment, because each one heard their own language being spoken. Utterly amazed, they asked:
>
> "Aren't all these who are speaking Galileans? Then how is it that each of us hears them in our native language? Parthians, Medes and Elamites; residents of Mesopotamia, Judea and Cappadocia, Pontus and Asia, Phrygia and Pamphylia, Egypt and the parts of Libya near Cyrene; visitors from Rome (both Jews and converts to Judaism); Cretans and Arabs—we hear them declaring the wonders of God in our own

tongues!" Amazed and perplexed, they asked one another, "What does this mean?" (Acts 2:1-12).

The Holy Spirit empowered the disciples to "declare the
wonders of God" in the languages represented in the crowd that
day because God was involved to enhance communication the
same way He was present to confuse communication in Genesis
11.

**Are you having any communication problems
with others, even though you speak the same language—
maybe even in your own family? Are you asking God to
help you communicate with others, especially as you
tell the story of His work in your life? Are you asking
God to help you not just hear but also fully comprehend
what others are trying to tell you?**

STUDY 22

BIG
GENESIS 12:1–5

We move on in this entry to one of the most important accounts in the Old Testament, for it is in chapter 12 that the Lord begins to fulfill the promise He made to Adam and Eve that their seed would crush the head of the serpent:

> The Lord had said to Abram, "Go from your country, your people and your father's household to the land I will show you. "I will make you into a great nation, and I will bless you; I will make your name great, and you will be a blessing. I will bless those who bless you, and whoever curses you I will curse; and all peoples on earth will be blessed through you." So Abram went, as the Lord had told him; and Lot went with him. Abram was seventy-five years old when he set out from Harran. He took his wife Sarai, his nephew Lot, all the possessions they had accumulated and the people they had acquired in Harran, and they set out for the land of Canaan, and they arrived there

(Genesis 12:1-5).

We do not know why the Lord called Abram, although it does seem like he had a heart for God even though he had no history in God of which we know. When the Lord revealed Himself to Abram, He continued His directive for the people to spread out, multiply, and fill the earth, something that those in Genesis 11 refused to do until they were forced to do so. Abram went willingly.

Put yourself in Abram's place. **How would you have received the news that you would be a great nation from your current situation? Would you ask a lot of questions? Would you want confirmation or more evidence that God was behind this?**

We are all comfortable with being small, but what if God wants you to be "big"? What is His plan for you is to start a business that will employ thousands, or launch a fashion or beauty line that carries your name, or perform on a big stage (singing, preaching, teaching, performing) that will touch many people as you encourage, inspire, instruct, or entertain them? If God wants you to be "big," then what do you have to do to make yourself equal to the task?

STUDY 23

A CREATIVE LIE
GENESIS 12:10-13, 17-20

In the last entry, we looked at Abram's call to be a great nation, which required that he leave his homeland and go to a place the Lord had set aside for him. During his journey, he and his wife Sarai entered the land of Egypt, where Abram became fearful:

> Now there was a famine in the land, and Abram went down to Egypt to live there for a while because the famine was severe. As he was about to enter Egypt, he said to his wife Sarai, "I know what a beautiful woman you are. When the Egyptians see you, they will say, 'This is his wife.' Then they will kill me but will let you live. Say you are my sister, so that I will be treated well for your sake and my life will be spared because of you" (Genesis 12:10-13).

When fear overcame him, Abram used his God-given creativity to concoct a lie, or what was really a half-truth, to protect himself. He excused what he did in his own mind, but

48

the king who took Abram's wife thinking she was his sister, knew that Abram had done wrong:

> But the Lord inflicted serious diseases on Pharaoh and his household because of Abram's wife Sarai. So Pharaoh summoned Abram. "What have you done to me?" he said. "Why didn't you tell me she was your wife? Why did you say, 'She is my sister,' so that I took her to be my wife? Now then, here is your wife. Take her and go!" Then Pharaoh gave orders about Abram to his men, and they sent him on his way, with his wife and everything he had (Genesis 12:17-20).

Truth is always better than a lie, even if that lie has its source in some measure of truth (Sarai was Abram's family member but also his wife). If you do not use your creativity for the right reasons, you will use it for the wrong reasons to devise clever rationalizations, usually called excuses, to explain why you are not doing what you are supposed to do. Excuses are often creative lies that soothe one's conscience and fend off critics, but at the end of the day, they are still lies that mask fear.

How have you anesthetized your conscience by using your creativity to justify your inaction (or wrong action)? Where do you need to accept responsibility for who you are and what you do so you can move on and God can bless you? What are your excuses to explain why you are not doing more for the Lord? Is it time that you stop using the best of your creativity to create a make-believe world and start using it to step out and move on as Abram did?

BUILDING ALTARS
GENESIS 12:6-8, 13:3-4, 14-18

As we examine the earlier years of Abram's life, we see he used his creativity to build an altar wherever he settled:

- Abram traveled through the land as far as the site of the great tree of Moreh at Shechem. At that time the Canaanites were in the land. The Lord appeared to Abram and said, "To your offspring I will give this land." So he built an altar there to the Lord, who had appeared to him (Genesis 12:6-7).

- From there he went on toward the hills east of Bethel and pitched his tent, with Bethel on the west and Ai on the east. There he built an altar to the Lord and called on the name of the Lord (Genesis 12:8).

- From the Negev he went from place to place until he came to Bethel, to the place between Bethel and Ai where his tent had been earlier and where he had first built an altar. There Abram

called on the name of the Lord (Genesis 13:3-4).
- So Abram went to live near the great trees of Mamre at Hebron, where he pitched his tents. There he built an altar to the Lord (Genesis 13:18).

Abram was pursuing the purpose God had assigned him, but the way was hard and fraught with uncertainty and danger. There was even conflict between him and his nephew, which caused them to split, Lot taking what appeared to be the best of the land when Abram allowed him to choose. At a time when it appeared Abram had experienced great loss, the Lord appeared to him and renewed His promises:

> The Lord said to Abram after Lot had parted from him, "Look around from where you are, to the north and south, to the east and west. All the land that you see I will give to you and your offspring forever. I will make your offspring like the dust of the earth, so that if anyone could count the dust, then your offspring could be counted. Go, walk through the length and breadth of the land, for I am giving it to you" (Genesis 13:14-17).

What was Abram's response after Lot left and the Lord spoke to him? He built an altar, using his hands and creativity to worship the Lord and recommit his way to the God who was leading him.

Your purpose and creativity are from the Lord and will only be fully expressed and realized in the context of worshiping the Lord. You are not alone nor are you strong or smart enough to fulfill God's purpose in your own understanding and strength. **Are you building your own kingdom or building altars of worship and sacrifice with your gifts, time, and talents? Is it time for you to build an altar and worship the Lord right where you are with what you have? Are you mindful of God's presence and leading in the midst of your success and failure as you carry out His assignment for you?** Remember, worship, and not success as your culture defines it, is the goal of your life's efforts.

MAKING WAR
GENESIS 14:13-16

The Spirit included an unusual story from the life of Abram in Genesis 14 that is worth examining as we consider the topics of purpose and creativity:

> Then one who had escaped came and told Abram the Hebrew, who was living by the oaks of Mamre the Amorite, brother of Eshcol and of Aner. These were allies of Abram. When Abram heard that his kinsman had been taken captive, he led forth his trained men, born in his house, 318 of them, and went in pursuit as far as Dan. And he divided his forces against them by night, he and his servants, and defeated them and pursued them to Hobah, north of Damascus. Then he brought back all the possessions, and also brought back his kinsman Lot with his possessions, and the women and the people (Genesis 14:13-16 ESV).

After Abram had allowed Lot to have first choice of the land he and his herdsmen would live in, Abraham had to go rescue his nephew. Consider these things as you reflect on this story:

1. Abram had 318 men in his household who could go to battle. That was quite an entourage from one man's household, showing Abram's wealth and organizational skills.

2. Not only did Abram have to oversee his personal enterprise, someone had to train those men how to fight and deploy for battle. Perhaps it was Abram or maybe he hired people specifically to carry out that task. The point is that he was proactive in preparing for the eventuality of conflict.

3. Abram had to go on the offensive to win back what his enemies had taken from him, even though Lot had exposed himself to this danger because of his selfish choice of the best land as he saw it.

4. Abram was confident he could lead that company into battle and defeat his enemies.

5. Abram displayed creativity in his attack plan. They marched by day and fought by night after Abram divided his forces in order to surprise and overwhelm his enemies.

6. Then Abram pursued his enemies for a distance after the battle until he had recovered his nephew along with their possessions, women, and children.

7. Abram was not afraid to go and fight for what was most important to him.

Are you willing to be creative and fight for what is most important to you, which may include not only your family but also your purpose and how it is being fulfilled? That may mean you are "fighting" to preserve your ministry, company, or creative expressions from enemies like recession, legal attacks, or people who are trying to steal what you have built. Sometimes your enemies are those you cannot see, for Paul reminded us that "for though we walk in the flesh, we are not waging war according to the flesh. For the weapons of our warfare are not of the flesh but have divine power to destroy strongholds" (2 Corinthians 10:3-4). Today is not a day to be passive but to stand and preserve and recover your purposeful creativity God has given you.

DOUBT AND DARKNESS
GENESIS 15:1-3, 7-8, 17

Even though God had given His promise to Abram, Abram went through a time of testing:

> After this, the word of the Lord came to Abram in a vision: "Do not be afraid, Abram. I am your shield, your very great reward." But Abram said, "Sovereign Lord, what can you give me since I remain childless and the one who will inherit my estate is Eliezer of Damascus?" And Abram said, "You have given me no children; so a servant in my household will be my heir" (Genesis 15:1-3).

Why do you think the Lord told Abram not to fear? It's because he was afraid! Even though God had spoken and proved Himself to him, Abram doubted what God had promised because he could not see how it would all come to pass.

Then if that wasn't enough, Abram went through what some call the dark night of the soul:

> He also said to him, "I am the Lord, who brought you out of Ur of the Chaldeans to give you this land to take possession of it." But Abram said, "Sovereign Lord, how can I know that I will gain possession of it?" (Genesis 15:7-8).

After Abram brought the Lord some sacrifices as God directed, we are told, "As the sun was setting, Abram fell into a deep sleep, and a thick and dreadful darkness came over him" (Genesis 15:12). Then we see that "when the sun had set and darkness had fallen, a smoking firepot with a blazing torch appeared and passed between the pieces" (Genesis 15:17).

When Abram was at his lowest and in the dark, God spoke to him and then provided light from the firepot and torch. God will do the same for you. Perhaps you are in doubt and darkness where your purpose or creativity are concerned. You have heard from the Lord and have faith, but you're afraid or maybe have even descended into depression. The word of the Lord for you is to trust Him. The less you feel or sense, the greater the need for faith.

Where are you in your faith walk where purpose and creativity are concerned? What doubts and fears do you have? The Lord is mindful of you and is willing to comfort and sustain you, even though your breakthrough may not be imminent. Today, embrace your darkness not as an end unto itself but as a means to seek the Lord and go to higher heights and deeper depths in Him. God has not forgotten you, but don't you forget Him or the promises He has made to you concerning His assignment for you.

CREATIVITY GONE AWRY
GENESIS 16:1–4

As we read another story from Abram's life, we read of the plan he and Sarai hatched so they could have a baby when it appeared no other way was possible:

> Now Sarai, Abram's wife, had borne him no children. But she had an Egyptian slave named Hagar; so she said to Abram, "The Lord has kept me from having children. Go, sleep with my slave; perhaps I can build a family through her." Abram agreed to what Sarai said. So after Abram had been living in Canaan ten years, Sarai his wife took her Egyptian slave Hagar and gave her to her husband to be his wife. He slept with Hagar, and she conceived (Genesis 16:1-4).

This may have been the custom of the land at that time, but it was not something the Lord had spoken to Abram to do.

When they got tired of waiting, the couple's creativity kicked in and they hatched a plan, which only had a 50-50 chance of succeeding because Hagar could have delivered a girl. Yet Abram and Sarai perhaps sincerely thought this was God's way to fulfill His promise to them. If they were sincere, they were sincerely wrong.

If you do not use your creativity for good, it will find its way to be expressed in activities that are not so good or help-ful. You will creatively manufacture excuses, fantasies, what-if scenarios, things to worry about, hobbies and activities, and op-tions to act and do *nothing* during your season of waiting. If not expressed properly, you may even use your creativity to produce an idol and then creatively justify its existence.

How are you expressing your creativity? Do you utilize it in the service of others and in the fulfillment of your purpose, or in producing excuses of why this is not the right time or you are not the right person for the task? Do you use it to creatively conceive of what faith step you can take with an idea you have or to conceive a reason why you should stay put and shut up?

The point is that you will use your creativity one way or another. Determine to use it for good in cooperation with God's plan for your life and not in a way that avoids the work and patience it takes to produce fruit in the will of God.

STUDY 28

AN AFFIRMATION
GENESIS 17:3-6

When Abram was 99 years old, the Lord appeared to him, and here is some of what happened:

> Abram fell facedown, and God said to him, "As for me, this is my covenant with you: You will be the father of many nations. No longer will you be called Abram; your name will be Abraham, for I have made you a father of many nations. I will make you very fruitful; I will make nations of you, and kings will come from you" (Genesis 17:3-6).

It is interesting that the Lord changed Abram's name, which is the first of a few name changes in biblical accounts. In this case, He changed it from Abram, which means exalted father, to Abraham, the father of a multitude. This happened while Abram had one son, Ishmael, whom he had sent away and before he and Sarai gave birth to Isaac, the son of promise.

How would you feel if you were childless and God wanted you to remember His promise of fruitfulness

every time someone said your name? Abraham had to walk in the truth of God's promise and not the truth of his reality, and it was God's doing. When Abraham spoke his own name, he was affirming God's promise and the faith reality he had walked in for many years. He would have a son who would be his heir and the first fruits of descendants as numerous as the sand on the seashore. To affirm is to "state as a fact or to assert strongly and publicly" and Abraham's name was indeed an affirmation of God's truth.

We are now called to walk in Abraham's footsteps and affirm God's truth of who we are even before that truth is evident to others—or to us. This is important where your purpose and creativity are concerned, for you must speak of both as though they already exist before they exist. Sounds foolish, doesn't it? Yet to say "I am a good writer" or "I run a successful business" is a statement of a future reality that begins in faith. It does not mean you have arrived, but it declares your destination, just as "I am father of a multitude" expressed Abraham's.

Second Corinthians 4:13 states, "'I believed; therefore I have spoken.' Since we have that same spirit of faith, we also believe and therefore speak." **Where do you need to adjust your speech to align with God's new reality for you? Where or how are you talking yourself out of who you will ultimately become? Can you no longer say, "I hope to be," or "Maybe one day I will," but instead say, "I am this or that"?** If you can, you will join with Abraham, Paul, Simon, Joseph (Barnabas), and others who had a name change long before the meaning of their new name became a reality.

GOD OPENS HAGAR'S EYES
GENESIS 21:14-19

Let's look at the first of many instances recorded in the Bible when God opened someone's eyes to see what they could not otherwise see:

Early the next morning Abraham took some food and a skin of water and gave them to Hagar. He set them on her shoulders and then sent her off with the boy. She went on her way and wandered in the Desert of Beersheba. When the water in the skin was gone, she put the boy under one of the bushes. Then she went off and sat down about a bowshot away, for she thought, "I cannot watch the boy die." And as she sat there, she began to sob. God heard the boy crying, and the angel of God called to Hagar from heaven and said to her, "What is the matter, Hagar?

Do not be afraid; God has heard the boy crying as he lies there. Lift the boy up and take him by the hand, for I will make him into a great nation." Then God opened her eyes and she saw a well of water. So she went and filled the skin with water and gave the boy a drink (Genesis 21:14-19).

Hagar found herself abandoned in the wilderness desert. We all know what a desert is like: hot in the day, cold at night, with no food or water. Hagar was convinced that, once their water ran out, her son was doomed to die a slow death—as was she. It was in the midst of her grief that the Lord broke in and spoke to her, promising that her son would not die but would rather become a great nation. After God directed her to take the boy by the hand, God opened her eyes and there she saw a well of water. My question is: **Did that well suddenly and miraculously appear from heaven or was it there all along?**

My own sense is that the well was there all along but Hagar could not see it. Why couldn't she see it? She was blind to its existence because of her thinking. After all, they were in the desert where everyone knows there is no water, so she could not see or even think to look for any. It's not that God had to heal her eyes, for there was nothing physically wrong with them. God had to change her thinking before she could see what was right in front of her all along.

What are the implications of this story for you? Where is your thinking preventing you from seeing your potential? Where have poverty thoughts caused you to be blinded to your riches in Christ? Where have ideas about your own limitations not allowed you to consider or pursue activities that are beyond what you think are your capabilities? Where have you even limited God because of your narrow or erroneous view of what He will and will not do?

The good news is that God wants to open your eyes. He did it for Hagar and she didn't even ask, so He will do it for you when you make the request, "Open my eyes, Lord, to see what

I am not seeing!" Pray that prayer today and then do like Hagar: Get up, take what your purpose and creativity by the hand, give it a drink of God's water, and then get about the work of making your ideas what God sees they can be instead of what you have limited them to be.

STUDY 30

"WE'LL BE BACK"
GENESIS 22:1-5

There is no end of fascinating stories involving Abraham and his walk of faith. In this study, we read,

> Some time later God tested Abraham. He said to him, "Abraham!" "Here I am," he replied. Then God said, "Take your son, your only son, whom you love— Isaac—and go to the region of Moriah. Sacrifice him there as a burnt offering on a mountain I will show you." Early the next morning Abraham got up and loaded his donkey. He took with him two of his servants and his son Isaac. When he had cut enough wood for the burnt offering, he set out for the place God had told him about. On the third day Abraham looked up and saw the place in the distance. He said to his servants, "Stay here with the donkey while I and the boy go over there. We will worship and then we will come back to you" (Genesis 22:1-5).

This is one of the more unusual stories in the Bible, for

God asked Abraham to sacrifice the very son God had given him, the son that represented God's promise to him that he would be a great nation. If God's promise was going to be fulfilled, Isaac had to live.

Notice how available Abraham was to the Lord. When God spoke, he said, "Here I am!" Someone once interpreted that to mean, "Sir, yes Sir!" Abraham did not say, "I'm busy" or "Later, Lord." Once God spoke to him, Abraham did not question or delay in carrying out God's request. He set out early in the morning on his journey, even though he did not know where he was going. After three days, Abraham saw the place. How did he know it was the right place? God must have confirmed it to him somehow, for Abraham knew and stopped.

The next phrase is what I want you to see. Abraham told his servants, "We are going over to worship and then *we will be back.*" He did not say, "I will be back." He did not say, "We hope to be back." He said, "We'll be back." Abraham knew he was going to sacrifice his son, but he also knew his son was the heir of promise, so he trusted that God was going to fulfill His promise by bringing Isaac back from the dead! The writer of Hebrews explained,

> By faith Abraham, when God tested him, offered Isaac as a sacrifice. He who had embraced the promises was about to sacrifice his one and only son, even though God had said to him, "It is through Isaac that your offspring will be reckoned." Abraham reasoned that God could even raise the dead, and so in a manner of speaking he did receive Isaac back from death (Hebrews 11:17-19).

Where do you need we'll-be-back faith that Abraham had? In what situation do you need to stand on what God promised where your purpose is concerned, the promise He made when He said, "That person is like a tree planted by streams of water, which yields its fruit in season and whose leaf does not wither—whatever they do prospers" (Psalm 1:3)? Where do you need to

respond like Abraham did—quickly and with urgency?
Abraham was not a perfect man, but in this story, he gave the perfect response—one all of us can learn from and apply to our own faith walk.

STUDY 31

ANOTHER ALTAR
GENESIS 22:6-10

In Study 24, we looked at the four altars built in response to the Lord's promises and presence in Abram's journey from the land of Ur to the land God had shown him was to be his. In this study, we look at another altar Abraham built, this one his fifth and most important:

Abraham took the wood for the burnt offering and placed it on his son Isaac, and he himself carried the fire and the knife. As the two of them went on together, Isaac spoke up and said to his father Abraham, "Father?" "Yes, my son?" Abraham replied. "The fire and wood are here," Isaac said, "but where is the lamb for the burnt offering?" Abraham answered, "God himself will provide the lamb for the burnt offering, my son." And the two of them went on together. When they reached the place God had told him about, Abraham built an altar there and arranged the wood on it. He bound his son Isaac and laid him on the altar, on top of the wood. Then he reached out his hand and took the knife to slay his son (Genesis 22:6-10).

This altar had to be big enough so Abraham could place Isaac on it and it was probably made of stone. The fire on this altar had to be sufficient to consume Isaac as a burnt offering so I would assume this was not a small altar as has been depicted by some modern renditions.

Abraham had to build all five altars in Genesis with his own hands, including this one, and God was also asking him to sacrifice his only son with those same hands. The lesson is that what you do through your purpose and with your creativity is ultimately for Him, no matter how many people you touch or serve. You must always keep your results in proper perspective and be willing to change course or surrender what you have been doing to His direction and will. Paul explained this dynamic in Jesus' life in his letter to the Philippians:

> In your relationships with one another, have the same mindset as Christ Jesus: Who, being in very nature God, did not consider equality with God something to be used to his own advantage; rather, he made himself nothing by taking the very nature of a servant, being made in human likeness. And being found in appearance as a man, he humbled himself by becoming obedient to death—even death on a cross! (Philippians 2:5-8).

Are you placing all you have and what is most important to you on the altar of worship in the service of others? Are you not only willing for God to take what you offer, but are you also building the altar—regularly and consciously willing to stop doing what it is that has become so meaningful to you as well as a source of godly fruit? Can you worship the Lord in times of loss or seasons of meager results as well as times of fulfilled promise and purpose plenty?

STUDY 32

WHAT'S IN A NAME?
GENESIS 22:13-14

In Study 8, we looked at the story of Adam naming the animals and pointed out it was an example of his God-given creativity. God directed Adam's work but Adam was free to name the animals whatever he chose. We see another example of this kind of creativity as we finish up our study of Abraham's sacrifice of Isaac in Genesis 22:

> Abraham looked up and there in a thicket he saw a ram caught by its horns. He went over and took the ram and sacrificed it as a burnt offering instead of his son. So Abraham called that place The Lord Will Provide. And to this day it is said, "On the mountain of the Lord it will be provided" (Genesis 22:13-14).

When Abraham found the ram, he saw the day of the Lord as Jesus described in John 8:56-59. At that moment, Abraham was standing on Mt. Moriah, the eventual location of the Temple in Jerusalem, where the ultimate sacrifice would take place through the death of Christ. When Abraham sacrificed the ram, he understood that God had sent a substitutionary sacrifice for Isaac, just like God would send His Son as the Lamb of God to be slain for the forgiveness of our sins. Then Abraham did something that Adam had also done: he used his creativity to define the moment.

Abraham assigned a name to God that is still used by the people of God. Abraham looked at the ram, sacrificed it, considered what had taken place, summarized what had happened in his mind, and called the place *Jehovah-Jireh: the Lord Will Provide*. Abraham saw that God would provide a sacrifice for Himself on His holy mountain and gave that place and God a new name. We do not see that God instructed Abraham to name the place. God did not say to him, "Name me now, according to what you have just seen." We certainly don't see that God was offended by what Abraham did. Abraham used his God-given ability to assess, evaluate and create, and in a few words summarized what could have taken many more words to adequately communicate—*The Lord Will Provide*.

God has given you the same capacity as Abraham had. **Where can you use your creativity to assess and create? Is it the name of your company? The title for your book? The trend in your field of work? An invention? A movement? A child? A nickname that will lovingly connect someone with their heritage or talent? Your sense of humor? Your ability to write, paint, sculpt, or rhyme?**

Who knows, maybe as you express your creativity, the identifying title you give something could become a lasting memorial to your creativity and God's work in your life—just like it did for Abraham. Then you can answer the question, "What's in a name?" by honestly saying, "The creativity God gave me is in that name." God will then be honored to be identified with your creativity, just as He was with Abraham's.

A PRAYER AND A PLAN
GENESIS 24:3-4, 10-16

God spared Abraham's son of promise named Isaac, but when it was time for Isaac to marry, Abraham had to exercise faith once again on his son's behalf:

> "I want you to swear by the Lord, the God of heaven and the God of earth, that you will not get a wife for my son from the daughters of the Canaanites, among whom I am living, but will go to my country and my own relatives and get a wife for my son Isaac" (Genesis 24:3-4).

Abraham commissioned his trusted servant with going to an unfamiliar land to find an unknown woman who would agree to come back with the servant to marry a man she had never met. That could have been labeled mission impossible, but the story does not indicate the servant hesitated or complained.

Instead, he saddled up and headed out to fulfill his master's command:

> Then the servant left, taking with him ten of his master's camels loaded with all kinds of good things from his master. He set out for Aram Naharaim and made his way to the town of Nahor. He had the camels kneel down near the well outside the town; it was toward evening, the time the women go out to draw water (Genesis 24:10-11).

What did he do when he got there? Did he put out the word and set up a series of interviews with potential candidates? Did he begin to ask around the area for references and leads? Did he put an ad in the local paper or post something on social media? (Of course, he didn't do that, but you get the idea). No, this faithful servant came up with a prayer and a plan:

> Then he prayed, "Lord, God of my master Abraham, make me successful today, and show kindness to my master Abraham. See, I am standing beside this spring, and the daughters of the townspeople are coming out to draw water. May it be that when I say to a young woman, 'Please let down your jar that I may have a drink,' and she says, 'Drink, and I'll water your camels too'—let her be the one you have chosen for your servant Isaac. By this I will know that you have shown kindness to my master" (Genesis 24:12-14).

The servant had faith, came up with a faith plan, and then prayed and turned his plan over to God. What was the result? The first woman who came to the well was the answer to his prayer:

> Before he had finished praying, Rebekah came out with her jar on her shoulder. She was the daughter of Bethuel son of Milkah, who was the wife of Abraham's brother Nahor. The woman was very beautiful, a virgin; no man had ever slept with her. She went down to the spring, filled her jar and came up again (Genesis 24:15-16).

Are you facing what you think are impossible tasks? Have you refused certain tasks because you considered them impossible? Then think again and take a lesson from this servant's handbook. Like he was, you should be creative, come up with a plan, pray, and then watch God move on your behalf. After all, you too are a servant of the Most High God. He has also given you an assignment to fulfill your purpose, but has not left you alone. He is present to help you do what He has assigned, but you must have the faith and apply your creativity to help make the assignment come to a successful conclusion.

STUDY 34

CONFLICTING INTERESTS
GENESIS 25:21-23

As we move on in our study, Abraham died and his son Isaac found that his wife, like his mother, had trouble conceiving a child. He prayed, God heard his prayer, and Rebekah became pregnant with twins. The babies were tussling with one another in her womb and we read that their activity was so unusual that Rebekah prayed for understanding:

> Isaac prayed to the Lord on behalf of his wife, because she was childless. The Lord answered his prayer, and his wife Rebekah became pregnant. The babies jostled each other within her, and she said, "Why is this happening to me?" So she went to inquire of the Lord. The Lord said to her . . . (Genesis 25:21-23).

Rebekah was carrying the purpose of Abraham's descendants but needed insight into the reason for her conflict within.

Notice that the Lord spoke to her and answered her prayers by giving her "inside" information to calm her heart and anxiety. Often, when you are creative or seeking purpose, there may be conflicting interests and feelings tussling inside of you, just like they were in Rebekah.

Perhaps you want to create, giving yourself to sculpting, painting, or writing, but you have a family to feed. Maybe you want to travel and do missions work, but your domestic responsibilities keep you grounded. Or perhaps you have a desire for ministry but don't see how you can afford to do that—or if you are even anointed or qualified to do so.

It is important to seek the Lord for wisdom but when you do, you must expect Him to respond and then you must act on what you hear. James wrote these words to help you sort through your conflicting interests or any other life scenario for which you need greater understanding:

> If any of you lacks wisdom, you should ask God, who gives generously to all without finding fault, and it will be given to you. But when you ask, you must believe and not doubt, because the one who doubts is like a wave of the sea, blown and tossed by the wind. That person should not expect to receive anything from the Lord. Such a person is double-minded and unstable in all they do (James 1:5-9).

Are you trying to resolve the conflict within or are you afraid of the answer so you make no effort to do so? When you pray, do you doubt the response, thus asking for more confirmation and prolonging your inner turmoil? Are you prepared that the response may lead to a change of lifestyle or occupation? Whatever the issue you are facing, it is important you obtain a clearer understanding so you can move on and give birth to the purpose and/or creativity of God you have been carrying that is causing conflict in your heart.

STUDY 35

MAKING ROOM
GENESIS 26:19-22

Isaac was not the most dynamic or charismatic man described in the Bible, but God still used him to continue Abraham's legacy. In Genesis 26, we read,

> Isaac's servants dug in the valley and discovered a well of fresh water there. But the herders of Gerar quarreled with those of Isaac and said, "The water is ours!" So he named the well Esek [*dispute*], because they disputed with him. Then they dug another well, but they quarreled over that one also; so he named it Sitnah [*opposition*]. He moved on from there and dug another well, and no one quarreled over it. He named it Rehoboth [*room*], saying, "Now the Lord has given us room and we will flourish in the land" (Genesis 26:19-22, meaning of words in brackets added by author].

Before he dug those three wells, Isaac was asked to leave his previous territory because he was too powerful and the locals feared his presence. So he left, only to encounter the opposition and dispute over the first two wells he dug to water his abundant flocks. Isaac kept moving on until he came to a place, dug a well, and found no opposition. He named that place Rehoboth because God had finally made a place or room for him.

The same can happen when you pursue your purpose. You can be a threat to others so you have to move on. Then you have some other successes, only to find that people oppose you yet again. This also happened to the Apostle Paul, for when he went to his beloved Jews, they did not want to hear from him. Yet when he went to the Gentiles, God opened doors and he was able to plant a church. Yet even after his success, opposition would arise which was Paul's eviction notice that it was time to move on to another field of work.

It is important to see in both instances of Isaac and Paul that God used opposition to direct their steps. He was sending them to a place where they were *celebrated* and not just *tolerated*, and when they got there, they both knew they were where they were supposed to be. God made room for them and he will do the same for you.

Are you ready to go where you are celebrated, or will you stubbornly stay and insist that where you are is where God must bless you? Do you see that it may not be a geographic relocation, but a shift to a different job, career, or people group that doesn't dread seeing you, welcoming you instead? Can you accept that even if you have failed, God will use it to take you away from those who only remember your failure and bring you to a people who don't know or care because you are God's answer to their prayers?

God wants you to know His will and the place where you will bear the most fruit. Therefore, don't fight His plan but rather go with the flow, confident God is sending you into situations where you are celebrated for who you are and what you bring and not resented for the same reasons.

STUDY 36

CUNNING CREATIVITY
GENESIS 27:5–10, 13

In Genesis 27, we read that Isaac was advanced in years and wanted to impart his blessing to his eldest son before he died. Jacob had already negotiated the purchase of his older brother's birthright but had to do something to also intercept his brother's blessing from their father. We read,

> Now Rebekah was listening as Isaac spoke to his son Esau. When Esau left for the open country to hunt game and bring it back, Rebekah said to her son Jacob, "Look, I overheard your father say to your brother Esau, 'Bring me some game and prepare me some tasty food to eat, so that I may give you my blessing in the presence of the Lord before I die.' Now, my son, listen carefully and do what I tell you: Go out to the flock and bring me two choice young goats, so I can prepare some tasty food for your father,

just the way he likes it. Then take it to your father to eat, so that he may give you his blessing before he dies" (Genesis 27:5-10).

Jacob's mother conspired with Jacob to trick Isaac into a blessing for Jacob through an elaborate ruse that had Jacob pretending to be Esau. This trick seemed to work and poor Isaac was humiliated when he found out he was hoodwinked by his own family!

When Jacob protested that if his father found out what she had done, he would curse instead of bless them, Rebekah replied, "My son, let the curse fall on me" (Genesis 27:13). It is of note that when Jacob had to flee his brother's anger after the plot was uncovered, Jacob never saw his mother alive again. The curse did indeed fall on her as it does on all who use their creativity to take matters into their own hands, trying to manipulate even God into doing what they want the way they want it.

Once again, the creativity God gave humans was perverted when Rebekah used it to devise a creative plot to steal and deceive. In a sense, Rebekah's creativity expressed itself as shrewdness or perhaps a better word is cunning. Instead of praying to the Lord to order the situation so the right son would get the correct blessing, she plotted and schemed.

We saw this same tendency to use God's creative gifts for personal gain in Abraham's life and here in Jacob's as well. **How are you using your creativity? Are you using it as God intends? Are you using it to carry out God's will or to circumvent it through creative excuse making? Are you stretching its limits by doing what is not easily discovered but inappropriate behavior for a believer (cheating on taxes, lying to gain some personal benefit, or staying silent when you receive a service or goods for which you did not pay)?** There is a price to pay whenever you do that, for God is watching, just like He was with Rebekah and Jacob. In the end, it is better to lose with integrity and ethics than win through cunning plans and schemes.

VIVID IMAGES
GENESIS 28:10-15

After Rebekah and Jacob tricked Isaac into giving his blessing to Jacob instead of Esau, Jacob had to leave town and take refuge with his uncle Laban to escape his brother's wrath. While on his way there, we learn that,

> Jacob left Beersheba and set out for Harran. When he reached a certain place, he stopped for the night because the sun had set. Taking one of the stones there, he put it under his head and lay down to sleep. He had a dream in which he saw a stairway resting on the earth, with its top reaching to heaven, and the angels of God were ascending and descending on it. There above it stood the Lord, and he said: "I am the Lord, the God of your father Abraham and the God of Isaac. I will give you and your descendants the land on which you are lying. Your descendants will be like the dust of the earth, and you will spread out to the west and to the east, to the north and to the south.

All peoples on earth will be blessed through you and your offspring. I am with you and will watch over you wherever you go, and I will bring you back to this land. I will not leave you until I have done what I have promised you" (Genesis 28:10-15).

Jacob realized the Lord was with him on his journey and made a vow to give God a tenth of all his increase if and when God brought him back to his father's household.

God painted a vivid picture to represent His presence in Jacob's life through a dream featuring a ladder with angels ascending and descending. He had given metaphors and similes to his grandfather that described his descendants as numerous as the sands on the shore and the stars in the sky. God often communicates through images and pictures to impart truth and values, and Jesus did the same through His parables and creative responses to questions.

What's more, while Jacob slept, he experienced one of our most fascinating human creative exercises: dreaming. When we sleep, there are aspects of us that are still awake and they generate and produce symbolic images, most of which we don't even remember. Yet research shows dreaming plays an important role in our psychological equilibrium.

Knowing God paints word pictures that create mental images, and keeping in mind that our dream machine functions every night, then **can you see the importance of using art to communicate and transmit what is important to us? Also, can you see that your creativity, like your dreaming, plays an important role in your mental health and harmony? Where can you tap into this aspect of your being to create vivid images in word or action that produce art, share your testimony, or teach others life lessons?**

STUDY 38

LOVE
GENESIS 29:16-20

Once Jacob left his homeland for his uncle's territory, he fell in love with his cousin Rachel and wanted to marry her:

> Now Laban had two daughters; the name of the older was Leah, and the name of the younger was Rachel. Leah had weak eyes, but Rachel had a lovely figure and was beautiful. Jacob was in love with Rachel and said, "I'll work for you seven years in return for your younger daughter Rachel." Laban said, "It's better that I give her to you than to some other man. Stay here with me." So Jacob served seven years to get Rachel, but they seemed like only a few days to him because of his love for her (Genesis 29:16-20).

Seven years went by quickly for Jacob because he was working for something he loved. When that happens to you that you find time going by quickly because of the joy you have in your activity, you can be sure you have found something connected to your purpose.

God is love so the best motivator for doing anything is love, whether it be love for another person, for God, or the joy of the activity itself. **What is it you do that when you do it, you can easily lose track of time? Playing the piano? Playing a particular sport? Studying? Helping the poor?** That love is an indication you are in the will of God and in a sense enter into an expression of eternity while you are engaged in that thing you love. The only love that does not work out so well is the love of money, for we read in First Timothy that it is the root of all evil.

Are you doing what you love as often as possible or do your days drag on? Do you welcome Fridays and dread Mondays or whatever day it is you must return to your work? Do you really believe it is God's best plan for you to hate your work? Find out what you love to do and then do it as often as possible and you will find the joy Jacob had when he labored for 2,555 days for what he loved. That's the kind of relationship you want to have with your work and that is the kind God wants you to have as well.

FOLLOWING THROUGH, CASHING IN
GENESIS 30:37–43, 31:10–13

When Jacob was preparing to leave Laban, his conniving father-in-law, Jacob further proposed a plan he would take all the spotted and speckled sheep as his payment for years of service. To Laban's surprise, Jacob proposed that all the existing spotted and speckled sheep be taken from the flock and only the yet-to-be-born spotted and speckled be Jacob's portion.

How could Jacob expect to gain any non-solid colored sheep if they were all removed before they could mate and reproduce? Laban was all too happy to comply with the plan and put a three-day's-journey distance between his flocks and Jacob's so there would be no possibility, or so he thought, of Jacob getting any of his sheep. But Jacob had a divine plan, a flash of brilliance and creative insight, that made him a wealthy man. We read in Genesis 30:37-43,

> Then Jacob took fresh rods of poplar and almond and plane trees, and peeled white stripes in them, exposing the white which *was* in the rods. He set the rods which he had peeled in front of the flocks in the gutters, *even* in the watering troughs, where the flocks came to drink; and they mated when they came to drink. So the flocks mated by the rods, and the flocks brought forth striped, speckled, and spotted. Jacob separated the lambs and made the flocks face toward the striped and all the black in the flock of Laban; and he put his own herds apart and did not put them with Laban's flock. Moreover, whenever the stronger of the flock were mating, Jacob would place the rods in the sight of the flock in the gutters, so that they might mate by the rods; but when the flock was feeble, he did not put *them* in; so the feebler were Laban's and the stronger Jacob's. So the man became exceedingly prosperous, and had large flocks and female and male servants and camels and donkeys.

This strategy seems a bit bizarre, but it worked. Later when Jacob was talking to his wives who were Laban's daughters, he said this about his plan in Genesis 31:10-13:

> And it came about at the time when the flock were mating that I lifted up my eyes and saw in a dream, and behold, the male goats which were mating *were* striped, speckled, and mottled. Then the angel of God said to me in the dream, 'Jacob,' and I said, 'Here I am.' He said, 'Lift up now your eyes and see *that* all the male goats which are mating are striped, speckled, and mottled; for I have seen all that Laban has been doing to you. I am the God *of* Bethel, where you anointed a pillar, where you made a vow to Me; now arise, leave this land, and return to the land of your birth.'"

God gave Jacob a creative strategy and prospered him through an idea. Jacob had to follow through on the idea to get his financial blessing. You can pray for money but when God answers, He may give you an idea. You have to convert that idea into action and only then does the money come. There are no shortcuts and no winning the lottery. Jacob got the creative inspiration, had to implement and follow through on what he saw, and over time he became wealthy.

Do you have any creative ideas you need to convert into action and then into cash and wealth? Are you following through on your heaven-inspired creativity? Do you even believe God wants to prosper you through the business or creative ideas you have?

STUDY 40

GOD IS IN THE FRUIT
GENESIS 30:37-43

In the previous study, we looked at the unusual strategy Jacob deployed to ensure his severance pay from his uncle would be sufficient to make him a rich man. Let's look at the strategy again:

> Then Jacob took fresh rods of poplar and almond and plane trees, and peeled white stripes in them, exposing the white which was in the rods. He set the rods which he had peeled in front of the flocks in the gutters, even in the watering troughs, where the flocks came to drink; and they mated when they came to drink. So the flocks mated by the rods, and the flocks brought forth striped, speckled, and spotted. Jacob separated the lambs, and made the flocks face toward the striped and all the black in the flock of Laban; and he put his own herds apart, and did not put them with Laban's flock. Moreover, whenever the stronger of the flock were mating, Jacob would

place the rods in the sight of the flock in the gutters, so that they might mate by the rods; but when the flock was feeble, he did not put them in; so the feebler were Laban's and the stronger Jacob's. So the man became exceedingly prosperous, and had large flocks and female and male servants and camels and donkeys (Genesis 30:37-43).

Commentators and scientists are at a loss to explain how this process could actually be effective and I will not try to explain it from a physiological point of view. We learned in Genesis 31 that God gave him this strategy as a means to compensate him for Laban's labor abuse. What was God doing or revealing when He showed this to Jacob?

It seems God had Jacob show the sheep a clear picture of what he wanted from them. Is that biblical or even practical? It is if you consider these truths:

1. A role model is a powerful teaching tool. Didn't Paul say to follow him as he followed Christ (see 1 Corinthians 11)? With his positive behavior in his followers' minds, there was a greater chance they would reproduce that behavior.

2. Paul quoted Jesus to have said, "Bad company corrupts good morals" (1 Corinthians 15:33). If that is true, then what does good company produce? It should reinforce and reproduce good moral behavior.

3. In Philippians 4:8-9, Paul wrote,

   "Finally, brothers and sisters, whatever is true, whatever is noble, whatever is right, whatever is pure, whatever is lovely, whatever is admirable— if anything is excellent or praiseworthy—think about such things. Whatever you have learned or received or heard from me or seen in me—put it into practice. And the God of peace will be with you."

> Notice that if the Philippians would set their minds on pure, right, and noble things—all things they had seen in Paul—and would then practice those things, they would have peace in their lives.

Once Jacob had done what he could do, then it was up to God to do His part, and that was to make the sheep fruitful so they would multiply as strong, healthy sheep. Once you set before you what you want or what God wants to produce through you, you have done your part. Then God has to be in the fruit or else there will be no fruit—but we know He wants you to be fruitful.

Are you spending time with people who are productive and have worthy behaviors worth imitating? Are you around people who are ethical and are not looking for shortcuts to financial or ministry success? Is your mind focusing on what it should—the pure, good, and righteous thoughts that will lead to peace?

The conditions above are not a magic formula, but rather conditions that must be met before the Lord will act on your behalf. If you are doing those things, then you can rest assured that God will do His part and ensure success, for God is indeed in the fruit.

STUDY 41

MORE ALTARS
GENESIS 32:1, 33:16-20, 35:1, 13-15

We have seen in past studies that Abraham built more than a few altars during his pilgrimage to and from the land God gave him. We did not look at Isaac's altar in Genesis 26:25, but we did examine the wells he dug, which were at the same venue where his altar was located (Rehoboth). Jacob followed more in his grandfather's footsteps and built multiple altars as well as give names to a few important areas on his journey home:

1. Jacob went on his way and the angels of God met him. When Jacob saw them, he said, "This is the camp of God!" So he named that place Mahanaim (Genesis 32:1).

2. So that day Esau started on his way back to Seir. Jacob, however, went to Sukkoth, where he built a place for himself and made shelters for his

livestock. That is why the place is called Sukkoth (Genesis 33:16-17) (note: he did *not* build an altar there).

3. After Jacob came from Paddan Aram, he arrived safely at the city of Shechem in Canaan and camped within sight of the city. For a hundred pieces of silver, he bought from the sons of Hamor, the father of Shechem, the plot of ground where he pitched his tent. There he set up an altar and called it El Elohe Israel (Genesis 33:18-20).

4. Then God went up from him at the place where he had talked with him. Jacob set up a stone pillar at the place where God had talked with him, and he poured out a drink offering on it; he also poured oil on it. Jacob called the place where God had talked with him Bethel (Genesis 35:13-15).

Note that the Lord did not tell Jacob what to name the areas, which resembles the story of Adam naming the animals. This indicates Jacob acted through his own free will, using the creativity and ability to think God gave him—just as Adam had done. It does not seem God was offended when either of them acted in that manner.

Yet there was one instance where God did tell Jacob to go back and build: "Go up to Bethel and settle there, and build an altar there to God, who appeared to you when you were fleeing from your brother Esau" (Genesis 35:1). God wanted Jacob to build to commemorate his encounter with God on his way to see his brother after a separation of many years. Jacob obeyed, built an altar, and had another encounter with God that led him to build the altar mentioned in number four above.

What we see in these examples is Jacob freely expressing his worship and creativity in each instance except for the one where God clearly directed him. **What are the implications of this pattern for you?** It seems that you may have more freedom to express your purpose than you have previously understood.

Are you waiting for God to direct your purpose and creativity, otherwise you refuse to do anything? Do you see God can and will direct you but not necessarily on every occasion? How will this impact your strategy and approach to your creative expressions and how you fulfill your purpose? Does this give you more freedom to be who God made you to be?

A CLEAR PURPOSE
GENESIS 37:5-11

As we continue our study of purpose and creativity in Genesis, let's see what lessons we can learn when we look at the life of young Joseph:

Joseph had a dream, and when he told it to his brothers, they hated him all the more. He said to them, "Listen to this dream I had: We were binding sheaves of grain out in the field when suddenly my sheaf rose and stood upright, while your sheaves gathered around mine and bowed down to it." His brothers said to him, "Do you intend to reign over us? Will you actually rule us?" And they hated him all the more because of his dream and what he had said. Then he had another dream, and he told it to his brothers. "Listen," he said, "I had another dream, and this time the sun and moon and eleven stars were bowing down to me." When he told his father as well as his brothers, his father rebuked him and said,

"What is this dream you had? Will your mother and I and your brothers actually come and bow down to the ground before you?" His brothers were jealous of him, but his father kept the matter in mind (Genesis 37:5-11).

Here are some purpose points and lessons to keep in mind as you pursue your own purpose:

1. **Joseph's purpose came looking for him**. God wants you to know your purpose more than you do. He often sends clues and signs for which you are not seeking but would do well to heed and interpret.

2. **Joseph was young when he discovered his purpose**. Joseph was to be the ruler in his family even though he was the next to youngest. Your childhood often holds indicators of your purpose. In a sense, you are never too young for purpose—to find, prepare for, or fulfill it.

3. **Joseph's purpose was confirmed in two dreams**. Joseph was going to need that reassurance and confirmation because of what he was about to go through. The clearer your call to purpose, the more you will need to hold on to that clarity in uncertain times.

4. **His brothers and his father understood what the dreams meant**. Often others can see your purpose more clearly than you do, so listen to what others say—but use that as a confirmation not as the final word. People can try to keep you from your purpose, just like Joseph's brothers did, so it's best to listen to others to hear purpose clues, but not rely on their endorsement.

Have you had a purpose revelation? Has it been confirmed? Are you thinking you are too young (or too old)? Are others being supportive or oppositional? Does

it seem like you have been in the preparation process to express your purpose for a long time? We will study Joseph for the next few studies, so learn from his example and determine you will be a person of purpose, just like he was—no matter how long it takes or what it costs.

STUDY 43

JOSEPH AND THE AMAZING TECHNICOLOR DREAMCOAT
GENESIS 37:3

In the last study, we began to look at the life of Joseph and saw that his father had blessed him with a special gift, one that caused his brothers to envy and hate Joseph all the more:

> Now Israel loved Joseph more than any of his other sons, because he had been born to him in his old age; and he made an ornate robe for him (Genesis 37:3).

Later, Joseph's brothers stripped him of the coat, soaked it in animal blood, and presented it to their father to cover their dirty deed of selling their brother into slavery.

The title of this study is not original. In fact, it is the title of a musical comedy with lyrics and music written by the famous Broadway team of Tim Rice and Andrew Lloyd Webber. In 1972, Rice and Webber premiered their show based on the story of Joseph from Genesis and it became a hit. Estimates are that more than 20,000 schools have presented their version of the production after the show had a successful run in New York and London. It is fascinating that Rice and Webber produced a show based on a Bible story and never mentioned God's name in the music or dialogue, but that is not the point of this study.

The point is that Rice and Webber had a creative idea and they acted on it. They produced something that became known the world over, a show that is still being staged in many places. The show was made into a movie and the musical has experienced numerous Broadway revivals.

Rice and Webber did not invent the Joseph story; they did not invent the musical or comedy; they did not introduce the world to stage productions. They simply acted on a creative impulse, adapting the story for modern consumption, writing the music, and finding the investors. The result was something thousands have enjoyed, perhaps not realizing they were captivated by one of the most intriguing stories in all of Scripture.

Do you have any creative ideas? Do you think they have to be ideas or concepts the world has never seen or heard? Do you have a dream to present the word of God to others through a creative expression like this show did? The only difference between you and the Rice/Webber team is they acted on their ideas, but you have not. It's time for you to stop talking yourself out of your ideas and start taking steps to make them happen. **There is no promise your ideas will become as big as** *Joseph and the Amazing Technicolor Dreamcoat* **did, but who's to say it won't**? The only way to find out is to do it. The rest is up to the Lord, but it all starts with you creating something God can use to touch the lives of others.

GEOGRAPHIC RIGHTEOUSNESS
GENESIS 39:2-4, 20-23

Genesis Joseph had two clear dreams that indicated to his family, and probably to him, that his destiny or purpose was to rule his family. I am sure they all had an idea of what that was going to look like, but always saw it in the context of their home territory and culture. Little did anyone know that Joseph's purpose would be fulfilled in a land far away as the vice president of the most powerful nation on earth.

When Joseph got to Egypt, how did he know he was in the right place and in God's will? How did he now it wasn't all over for him? The Bible tells us more than once that God was with him:

> The Lord was with Joseph so that he prospered, and he lived in the house of his Egyptian master. When his master saw that the Lord was with him and that the Lord gave him success in everything he did,

Joseph found favor in his eyes and became his attendant. Potiphar put him in charge of his household, and he entrusted to his care everything he owned (Genesis 39:2-4).

But while Joseph was there in the prison, the Lord was with him; he showed him kindness and granted him favor in the eyes of the prison warden. So the warden put Joseph in charge of all those held in the prison, and he was made responsible for all that was done there. The warden paid no attention to anything under Joseph's care, because the Lord was with Joseph and gave him success in whatever he did (Genesis 39:20b-23).

Joseph had a purpose but that purpose could only be fulfilled in Egypt, not in the place he called home. He could not be righteous in God's will in the land of his fathers when his purpose had to be fulfilled in Egypt. Geography came into play in Joseph's life and it may be a factor in yours, too. God confirmed where Joseph was to be. When he was at home, there was no favor of God—only turmoil. When he went to Egypt, God prospered and blessed him—even when he was serving time in prison.

Your purpose may also be clear, but you are not experiencing God's favor. That could be because you are missing what I have labeled "geographic righteousness." That doesn't mean you have to relocate to another area (that's possible), but you may have to stop trying to make something happen where you are, and look for a new church, company, people group, city, or nation where you will be welcomed with open arms. For me, that area was and is Africa where I always sense God's favor when I am there. When I am at home, I don't have near the impact I do when I am in Kenya or Zimbabwe,

Where are you supposed to be? Are you trying to make a go of it where you have been only to experience rejection and indifference? Have you visited someplace (for instance, a people group, folks with a physical

or mental challenge) where you sense God's favor and help? Are you ready to stop trying to make something happen and go where something happens? I urge you to consider this concept of geographic righteousness and look for a place where you are welcomed and celebrated and not just tolerated.

STUDY 45

NO BIG DEAL
GENESIS 41:14-16, 28

Once Joseph arrived in Egypt, he served a man named Potiphar but found himself in jail after the man's wife falsely accused him of sexual misconduct. While in jail, Joseph interpreted dreams for two of Pharaoh's officials, hoping his help would secure his release. Two years later, one of the officials told Pharaoh about Joseph when Pharaoh was looking for someone to interpret his dreams. We read,

> So Pharaoh sent for Joseph, and he was quickly brought from the dungeon. When he had shaved and changed his clothes, he came before Pharaoh. Pharaoh said to Joseph, "I had a dream, and no one can interpret it. But I have heard it said of you that when you hear a dream you can interpret it" (Genesis 41:14-15).

In a matter of minutes, Joseph moved from the dungeon to the king's palace and was standing before the most powerful man in the world. First, he had to be made presentable and then he was confronted with the command performance to tell Pharaoh what his dreams meant. How would you respond? Would you be nervous? Feel pressure? Wonder what would happen to you if you could not give the king what he wanted?

How did Joseph respond? He responded by saying in essence it was no big deal: "'I cannot do it,' Joseph replied to Pharaoh, 'but God will give Pharaoh the answer he desires'" (Genesis 41:16). What courage! What faith! What composure and confidence! How did Joseph know God wanted to provide the meaning? How did he know he would hear and relate it properly? As Joseph stood before Pharaoh and shared the interpretation, he said, "It is just as I said to Pharaoh: God has shown Pharaoh what he is about to do" (Genesis 41:28). In other words, Joseph was saying, "I told you it's no big deal at all to do this."

That is how purpose operates in your life as well. You do something and others may marvel, but you think, "That's no big deal; it was pretty easy." I had a friend who used to stand before a crowd of thousands and say, "Let's write a worship song." He would then ask for a passage, a key, a tempo, and have the band start playing. When he was done, he and they had composed a song.

What do you do that's "no big deal"? What can you produce, create, or devise that would take others a long time—if they could do it at all? Where does God work with you so that others, like Pharaoh's official, remember and recommend you to their friends or associates?

The reason you can do this is for the same reason Joseph gave: "I can't do it, but God can." It's what Paul wrote in 1 Corinthians 15:10: "But by the grace of God I am what I am, and his grace to me was not without effect. No, I worked harder than all of them—yet not I, but the grace of God that was with me." Don't try to explain or ignore this phenomenon in your life. Just go with the flow and produce results just like Joseph did, whether you are doing it for a few people behind bars or the most important man in the world.

STUDY 46

A DREAM REMEMBERED
GENESIS 37:1-2, 41:46, 42:6-9, 45:6

In the last study, we saw that Joseph was made regent over Egypt, second in command with only Pharaoh above him. According to Joseph's interpretations of Pharaoh's dreams, there were to be seven good years of plenty and then seven bad years of famine. Let's do some math to determine how old Joseph was during his Egyptian service and when he was reunited with his brothers:

- Joseph was 17 when he had his dreams that his brothers and parents would bow to him as their leader (see Genesis 37:1-2).

- Joseph served Potiphar and the jailer for 13 years, which made him 30 when he became Egypt's chief administrator (see Genesis 41:46).

- There were seven good years as Joseph had predicted, which means he was 37 when the famine began.

Then we read,

> Now Joseph was the governor of the land, the person
> who sold grain to all its people. So when Joseph's
> brothers arrived, they bowed down to him with their
> faces to the ground. As soon as Joseph saw his broth-
> ers, he recognized them, but he pretended to be a
> stranger and spoke harshly to them. "Where do you
> come from?" he asked. "From the land of Canaan,"
> they replied, "to buy food." Although Joseph recog-
> nized his brothers, they did not recognize him. Then
> he remembered his dreams about them and said to
> them, "You are spies! You have come to see where
> our land is unprotected" (Genesis 42:6-9).

We later find out that his brothers came to him the second time in the second year of the famine: "For two years now
there has been famine in the land, and for the next five years
there will be no plowing and reaping" (Genesis 45:6). That
means Joseph was 39 years old when he revealed himself to
them.

Go back to Genesis 42:8: "Then he remembered the
dreams about them." Now, consider this question: How could
Joseph remember the dreams he had when he was 17 for 22
years when you can't remember your dreams from last night?
For 22 years, Joseph had to live in those dreams, hold on to
those dreams, wrestle with those dreams, remind God of those
dreams, and remind himself of those dreams when it seemed
like all was lost.

If you are going to be a person of purpose who expe-
riences success, you probably have some dreams, maybe even
some big ones. You can be sure you will be tested to see if
you can hold on to them and act faithfully when it seems like
those dreams are as far away from you as the sun is from the
Earth. Joseph changed history and fulfilled God's plan because
he held on to his dreams on the way down to Egypt as a slave,
in his master's house as the man's wife urged him to enter into

an illicit affair, in prison in his darkest nights, during the two years when the cupbearer forgot Joseph's kindness, and during seven years of plenty. Then one day, when he least expected it to happen, his brothers came into his presence and bowed down.

What is your purpose or creative dream? What do you want to see accomplished in your lifetime? Are you being tested? Far away from their fulfillment? If you are discouraged or just need a reminder that God is watching, then consider Joseph, who held on to his dream for more than two decades, only to see it fulfilled in a matter of minutes. God is still orchestrating your destiny so keep those dreams alive by whatever means possible.

THE GOOD PHARAOH
GENESIS 47:5-6

The Pharaoh in Joseph's story doesn't get enough recognition for the excellent leader he was. The reasons he was so effective are many:

1. He put the cupbearer and baker on probation rather than dismiss them immediately.

2. In the long run, he retained the cupbearer and "fired" the baker, which proved to be wise since the cupbearer introduced him to Joseph.

3. He knew how to recognize talent for he hired Joseph on the spot.

4. He gave Joseph unlimited authority to do his job of storing grain as he saw fit.

5. He took care of Joseph, making sure he had a wife and all he needed to be successful.

Pharaoh once again showed his leadership ability when Joseph's family arrived from Canaan to stay in Egypt. He did not promise he would employ all Joseph's family, but instead said this:

> Pharaoh said to Joseph, "Your father and your brothers have come to you, and the land of Egypt is before you; settle your father and your brothers in the best part of the land. Let them live in Goshen. And if you know of any among them with special ability, put them in charge of my own livestock" (Genesis 47:5-6).

Pharaoh was not "into" nepotism, hiring people based on who they were related to. He only wanted those who had "special ability." In other words, he was directing Joseph to hire his brothers if they were skilled at what they did. Otherwise, Pharaoh was willing to provide for his family but not give them a job. The real issue is that Pharaoh built his empire on the strengths of his people and not his whims or preferences. That meant his people had to know what their strengths were so they could serve Pharaoh and Egypt effectively.

What are your strengths? What do you do best? Do you know your spiritual gifts? If you are a leader, do you know the strengths of the people with whom you work? Do you promote who is already in your organization according to what they are able to do? Have you hired your family based on merit or relationship? Learn from Pharaoh and hire the best people, and if you have trouble recognizing who they are, get someone to help you.

FAMINE FINANCES
GENESIS 47:15-21, 23-26

Joseph had predicted the seven years of famine, preparing for them by laying up grain in the good years. But then he encountered a problem:

> When the money of the people of Egypt and Canaan was gone, all Egypt came to Joseph and said, "Give us food. Why should we die before your eyes? Our money is all gone." "Then bring your livestock," said Joseph. "I will sell you food in exchange for your livestock, since your money is gone." So they brought their livestock to Joseph, and he gave them food in exchange for their horses, their sheep and goats, their cattle and donkeys. And he brought them through that year with food in exchange for all their livestock (Genesis 47:15-17).

The Egyptian government went into the grocery business and sold people the food that was in storage. When their money and livestock ran out and they had no way to pay, Joseph did this:

When that year was over, they came to him the following year and said, "We cannot hide from our lord
the fact that since our money is gone and our livestock belongs to you, there is nothing left for our
lord except our bodies and our land. Why should we
perish before your eyes—we and our land as well?
Buy us and our land in exchange for food, and we
with our land will be in bondage to Pharaoh. Give
us seed so that we may live and not die, and that the
land may not become desolate." So Joseph bought
all the land in Egypt for Pharaoh. The Egyptians,
one and all, sold their fields, because the famine was
too severe for them. The land became Pharaoh's, and
Joseph reduced the people to servitude, from one end
of Egypt to the other. . . Joseph said to the people,
"Now that I have bought you and your land today
for Pharaoh, here is seed for you so you can plant the
ground. But when the crop comes in, give a fifth of
it to Pharaoh. The other four-fifths you may keep
as seed for the fields and as food for yourselves and
your households and your children." . . . So Joseph
established it as a law concerning land in Egypt—still
in force today—that a fifth of the produce belongs to
Pharaoh. It was only the land of the priests that did
not become Pharaoh's (Genesis 47:18-21, 23-24, 26).

While he was careful to make his boss a lot of money, Joseph kept nothing for himself. He accepted no bribes or
kickbacks. He took care of the people even though he taxed
the people at a fair rate (20%). (Some dispute that Joseph did
good in this situation and claimed he actually enslaved the people, enriching Pharaoh in the process. We will not debate that
position here.) The people seemed grateful and declared, "'You
have saved our lives,' they said. 'May we find favor in the eyes of
our lord; we will be in bondage to Pharaoh'" (Genesis 47:25).

**How creative are you when you face problems at
work or in ministry you have never before encountered?**

Do you take care of the people or yourself? Do the people bless you for your role or speak ill of you? Does your presence benefit those who have employed you? Do you bring glory to God in what you do and how you do it?

DEATHBED BLESSING
GENESIS 48:12-14

When Jacob, renamed Israel, was dying, Joseph took his sons to him to receive their grandfather's blessing. This is reminiscent of Jacob and Esau paying a similar visit to their father, Isaac, except that Rachel and Jacob conspired to steal the elder's blessing. Joseph perhaps knew the story and so he positioned his elder son at Jacob's right hand and Ephraim, his youngest, at Jacob's left so the elder could get the right hand of blessing. Jacob did not cooperate with Joseph's plan but instead we read,

> Then Joseph removed them from Israel's knees and bowed down with his face to the ground. And Joseph took both of them, Ephraim on his right toward Israel's left hand and Manasseh on his left toward Israel's right hand, and brought them close to him. But Israel reached out his right hand and put it on Ephraim's head, though he was the younger, and crossing his arms, he put his left hand on Manasseh's head, even though Manasseh was the firstborn (Genesis 48:12-14).

This time, Jacob got it right and acted as a prince, the meaning of his new name, Israel. There was no conniving, no plots, no stealing. Jacob imparted the greater blessing to the younger, as had been bestowed upon him, but without the intrigue or resulting family feud.

Why did Israel give the greater blessing to Ephraim and not Manasseh? He did so because he finally realized why he received the blessing instead of his brother, Esau. Jacob got the blessing because of God's grace. It was God's choice to bless Jacob so he was then cooperating with God's plan to pass the grace on to another undeserving person. Ephraim, whose name literally means "God has made me fruitful," was appointed by God to be greater than his brother. There was no natural reason for that choice; it was only a matter of God's sovereign will. It is interesting that every time after this when the tribes were numbered, Ephraim's head count was always greater than his brother's. Why? It was only because of God's grace.

Do you realize that you have a purpose, gifts, and creative skills for no other reason than God chose to give them to you? They are a token of God's grace toward you and those who will benefit as you deploy them. **Do you also realize that you can receive God's grace in vain?** "As God's co-workers we urge you not to receive God's grace in vain" (2 Corinthians 6:1). **Are you doing something with the grace extended you? Are you bearing fruit? Are you passing grace blessings on to others?**

BEAUTIFUL BLESSINGS
GENESIS 49:2, 8-12, 27

As we approach the end of Genesis, we have the account of the blessings Jacob pronounced on his sons after he had bestowed a special blessing on Joseph's sons, his grandsons Manasseh and Ephraim: "Assemble and listen, sons of Jacob; listen to your father Israel" (Genesis 49:2). He pronounced the longest and choicest blessings on two of his twelve sons, Judah and Joseph. Let's look at Joseph's blessing:

> "Judah, your brothers will praise you; your hand will be on the neck of your enemies; your father's sons will bow down to you. You are a lion's cub, Judah; you return from the prey, my son. Like a lion he crouches and lies down, like a lioness—who dares to rouse him? The scepter will not depart from Judah, nor the ruler's staff from between his feet, until he to whom it belongs shall come and the obedience of the nations shall be his. He will tether his donkey to a vine, his colt to the choicest branch; he will wash

his garments in wine, his robes in the blood of grapes. His eyes will be darker than wine, his teeth whiter than milk" (Genesis 49:8–12).

When reading any of the blessings, including Judah's, the reader is confronted with some thoughtful phrases filled with beautiful images and elegant words. Jacob must have given a lot of thought to what he said, and it seems he spoke in front of all the sons, not meeting with them one on one even if he did not have pleasant things to predict concerning their futures. Yet the only tribes that seemed to maintain their prominence into the time of Jesus were Judah, Joseph and Mary's tribe, and Benjamin, which was the heritage of the Apostle Paul.

It is interesting that the prediction concerning the tribe of Benjamin was fulfilled in Paul's life as a missionary: "Benjamin is a ravenous wolf; in the morning he devours the prey, in the evening he divides the plunder" (Genesis 49:27). In a sense, Jacob wasn't just blessing his sons; he was prophetically addressing the good things to come from his bloodline in Christ.

Are you pronouncing blessings on your family and those closest to you? Do you spend time thinking about how you can bless them through written or spoken words? Are you watching and helping to guide the will and purpose of God in those you love? Do you see that God has an individual purpose for your family members and that you are to help foster and promote that purpose? What more can you do to declare beautiful blessings on others?

STUDY 51

THE BIG PICTURE
GENESIS 39:9, 40:24-25,
41:16, 50:19-20

We do not know very much about Joseph's spiritual life. He didn't write psalms like David or see visions of the future like Daniel did. He was simply a magnificent administrator whom God used to save the world. We know God spoke to Joseph through dreams. When Potiphar's wife wanted to seduce him, Joseph responded, "No one is greater in this house than I am. My master has withheld nothing from me except you, because you are his wife. How then could I do such a wicked thing and sin against God?" (Genesis 39:9).

When he came before Pharaoh, he said, "'I cannot do it,' Joseph replied to Pharaoh, 'but God will give Pharaoh the answer he desires'" (Genesis 41:16). He then married an Egyptian priest's daughter and did not mention God again until the last chapter of Genesis. When his brothers feared for their lives after their father died, Joseph said, "Don't be afraid. Am I in the place of God? You intended to harm me, but God intended it for good to accomplish what is now being done, the saving of many lives" (Genesis 50:19-20).

It was when Joseph died, however, that he revealed the secret of his success and why he was able to survive and then prosper in Egypt. He did so because he had faith and as he died shared words of faith that described the big picture of what God was going to do for His people:

> Then Joseph said to his brothers, "I am about to die. But God will surely come to your aid and take you up out of this land to the land he promised on oath to Abraham, Isaac and Jacob." And Joseph made the Israelites swear an oath and said, "God will surely come to your aid, and then you must carry my bones up from this place" (Genesis 40:24-25).

We then read in Exodus 13:19 of what Moses did centuries after Joseph made the Israelites promise to bury him in the Promised Land: "Moses took the bones of Joseph with him because Joseph had made the Israelites swear an oath. He had said, 'God will surely come to your aid, and then you must carry my bones up with you from this place.'"

Do you see God's hand in your past even when people wronged or betrayed you? Do you acknowledge God as the One who helps you fulfill your purpose as Joseph did? Do you have the big picture of what God is doing in your life with your purpose and creativity? Do you speak words of faith not only about your present but your future, even after you're gone? Are you creating and working with the realization that God can preserve and use what you do even after you are gone from this life? What faith legacy do you want to leave for your posterity?

ABOUT
JOHN W. STANKO

John founded a personal and leadership development company, called *PurposeQuest*, in 2001 and today travels the world to speak, consult and inspire leaders and people everywhere. From 2001-2008, he spent six months a year in Africa and still enjoys visiting and working on that continent. Most recently, John founded Urban Press, a publishing service designed to tell stories of the city, from the city and to the city. John is the author of 50 books.

KEEP IN TOUCH WITH JOHN W. STANKO

www.purposequest.com
www.johnstanko.us
www.stankobiblestudy.com
www.stankomondaymemo.com

or via email at johnstanko@gmail.com

John also does extensive relief and
community development work in Kenya.
You can see some of his projects at
www.purposequest.com/contributions

PurposeQuest International
PO Box 8882
Pittsburgh, PA 15221-0882

ADDITIONAL TITLES
BY JOHN W. STANKO